Look Back With Love

Books by Alberta Pierson Hannum

Spin a Silver Dollar

Thursday April

The Hills Step Lightly

The Gods and One

The Mountain People
  in *The Great Smokies and the Blue Ridge*

Paint the Wind

Roseanna McCoy

Look Back With Love

A Recollection of the Blue Ridge

BY ALBERTA PIERSON HANNUM

The Vanguard Press, Inc · *New York*

Manufactured in the United States of America
Designer: Ernst Reichl

Standard Book Number 8149–0007–0
Library of Congress Catalog Card Number: 70–89659

> "*Let the mountains and the hills
> bring a message of peace
> to the people.*"
>
> —Book of Psalms
> (THE JERUSALEM BIBLE)

There is no question at all
about the dedication of this book.
It could not possibly have been written
without the clear-seeing editorial help
of my delighted-in family.

Author's Note: This is a personal remembrance of a time that was, and perhaps will never be again—of mountain friends, and of nights with a startlingly bright single star low in the sky —guiding or marking the end: nights not of question but of wonder.

And if this is a different look at the Appalachian people, it is also a challenge to look at the basic American dream.

Acknowledgment

The author is warmly grateful to her friend, Mrs. Crate Carpenter, for her trusting permission to use some of Jacob Carpenter's diary entries as chapter headings.

Table of Contents

List of Illustrations

Look Back With Love

A *Stroke* of *Genius*

MOUNTAINS are like music, the great kind of music that is everything you have ever known about and something more. They are a powerful music that rolls up from the earth. The southern mountains begin their particular theme along the Potomac, quietly, swelling into long full rolls of South Branch harmony. Nothing is out of line or out of tune there. Then, abruptly, like a stroke of genius, you have the roughs of the Virginias and Kentucky, mounting and slashing but just right— there, nothing else would have done. And before you can quite regain your composure, the whole thing sweeps together into wild, almighty crescendos, Tennessee and the Carolinas pushing their forested lofts up and up and up into intense blue sky! Then, worn and satisfied, the motif goes off quietly again, into Alabama and Georgia.

Eight states with music in their earth. Eight states of a people with music in their words and lives—as curious a combination of the mellowed-old and harshly new as their mountains are distinctive from any others.

The Great Smokies and the Blue Ridge especially were old before the Rockies or the Andes were born. Upon them in after ages were cradled the first of the American hardwoods, towering giants that roar in the wind and whisper mysteriously in the rain. John Muir, the noted naturalist, once said of these trees, "However slighted by man, they must have been a great delight to God, for they are the best He ever planted." And the remarkable race of people who carved an empire out of that slighted wilderness probably have been more caricatured, with less actually known about them, than any other single group of people in the world.

But there was a man, Jacob Carpenter, who lived on Three Mile Creek just under the crest of the Blue Ridge, who knew them from the inside, for he was one of them. And Uncle Jake, as he is familiarly remembered in that high country, kept a diary.

It is a unique sort of diary, for it is done in the old European fashion of Tanagra, the placing on graves of miniature clay figures in poses representing the departed's earthly activities. When someone in Uncle Jake's community died, he made note of it in a red-backed account ledger. The name, the date—then he added his frank opinion of the deceased's way of living.

"Jake warn't no scribe," one of his neighbors said. True. The trenchant entries are all but illegible and he had his own ideas about spelling. Yet the diary is important. Its dates, for one thing —starting with the death of a Revolutionary War soldier and ending after the first World War—cover the whole span of our highlanders' existence as a separate people. For another, although it is a record of only a small section of the southern Appalachian mountains that slash their way southwest, it is characteristic of communities all through the range.

And when Jacob Carpenter added his own name—"Jacob Carpenter took down sick April 1 1919"—that ledger contained a rare record of the prolific vigor, the courage and self-reliance that has been in America since the beginning, that Uncle Jake's people helped to bring in. Jacob Carpenter left a guide to an earthy humor, and a mental calmness that can help steady a nation's thinking.

That Fighting Thing Called Freedom

Wm Davis age 100.8 dide oc 5 1841
war old solder in rev war and got his
thie brok in last fite in kings monton he
war farmer and made brandy and never
had drunker in family.

WILLIAM Davis was a Pennsylvanian. During the Revolution he was with that part of Washington's troops who got into North Carolina. One day when the camp ran out of food, he was sent out with a foraging party for game. When he got up into the mountains, he thought it was the prettiest country he had ever seen.

I happened to hear this about William Davis at the top of Linville Mountain, with the Linville River too directly below to see and too far down to hear. But the opposite side of the gorge does not drop sheer. It lies back, full and lush with all the greens there are—wide with unplungeable depths of woods. And away and beyond reach miles and miles of sun and shadow, with the shadow at some indefinable place becoming blue mountain and then gray mountain until it is hard to say which is gray cloud and which gray mountain. There is no one thing the eye can get hold of. But all the senses grow lulled as you look, and at the same time heightened. I could understand how William Davis had thought it was pretty country.

"Of course," explained the old-timer who was telling me the story, "hit war the b'ar and the deer made hit so purty to him."

At any rate, whether from the aesthete's or the hunter's view, he liked it, and he swore right then and there that if he lived through the war, he was going back to Pennsylvania and get him a woman and come there and live. And he did.

In some such way, almost all mountain-family histories go back at least as far as the Revolution.

"The first of my folks to come," a North Carolinian woman told me, "come over to fight for the King." She was a woman with an evident amount of spunk about her. She was sitting on a low-legged hickory chair on her porch, her feet planted substantially wide so her aproned knees could clamp a big wooden bowl of red apples she was peeling for apple butter. Occasionally she'd lift the end of the apple knife and scratch her nose.

"But when he got hyur," she said, "he saw the Colonists were bein' imposed upon, so he swapped sides and started fightin' for America. And," she finished dryly, "that contrary streak still kindly runs through our family."

Most highlanders can trace their beginnings back even farther. One old man in Tennessee obligingly took his ancestry clear back to Christopher Columbus. He 'lowed that *his* folks had come over with Christopher Columbus on an old sail ship. "But when they got hyur they got kindly wild, and tuk to follerin' the game, a-wanderin' to and fro, till the generations they all evaporated, and the only ones of 'em that war left war them with strength enough to climb up into the hills."

Despite the Christopher Columbus part of it, the rhythmic recital has an element of soundness in it. No doubt many of them did come over on an "old sail ship." There is a record of the *Eagle Wing* setting sail from Ireland as early as 1636, filled with the Scotch-Irish Presbyterians who were destined to become highlander forebears.

The story of our southern mountain people never has been set

down fully in history. You can piece it together only from incidental bits in the copious records of the early New England and
seacoast colonies, and from old church records, family histories,
and biographies. However, in the main, the story of their being is
very much like that of America itself—the story of people daring
to leave the known and fare forth into the unknown in search of
religious and political freedom.

In the beginning, in 1607, James I transplanted Scotch and
English Presbyterians to the northern counties of Ireland and
called them Scotch-Irish, although they never got along with the
Irish. A quick-tempered, visionary, highly independent people,
they also quarreled violently with the British Crown. It has been
said that their fear of God was so great it left in them no fear of
mortal man.

Early in the eighteenth century they left the old country entirely and came in large numbers to America. But upon arrival at
the new shores, they found the seacoast crowded and many of
the same conditions there that they had left at home. Impatiently
they pushed on westward, to the frontier borders of Pennsylvania, beyond the Palatine Germans and the English already settled there. A great many went into the Valley of Virginia. But
there, especially, the Church of England was firmly established,
and again they found themselves forced to worship in a way to
which they were unsympathetic. Furthermore, they were heavily taxed and received little in return.

Again they moved on—southward along the Cumberland Valley, westward into the Shenandoah: the determined Scotch-Irish
picking up a strong lot of the Palatine Germans, intermarrying
with the English, being joined by a few French Huguenots and
Swiss—their numbers mounting, their power snowballing. They
were becoming an element to be taken into consideration in the
new colonies. The consideration was that the King's law spared
no pains to bring them to heel. But it was not in their history to
back off weakly before authority. So once more they pushed on,
in further search of that elusive thing called freedom.

After the acquisition of territory west of the Alleghenies from the French in 1763, England, to prevent her colonial population from scattering, put out a proclamation forbidding emigration beyond the mountains. To this proclamation the Scotch-Irish and their friends and relatives paid not the slightest attention. Consequently, by the time of the actual outbreak of the Revolution, that "western" territory had been well explored and hunted, and settlements had been begun.

But still they found themselves coming short of their ideal of religious and political freedom. With their numbers scattering to remote hollows in the mountain wilderness, church services naturally grew infrequent, and the churches and schoolhouses they built side by side wherever they settled were now few. However, the long arm of the King's law still reached them. They were still being governed according to colonial precedent in the lowlands that—according to a positive old man who remembered an opinionated grandfather who was in the Revolution—"didn't have a continental to do with the way things was up in the mountains!" Heavy taxes for a government in which they had no part were still being imposed. That they felt this was unfair is shown by a few old records of formal resolutions of rebellion against "paying any officer any more fees than the law allows, unless we are obliged to do it; and then to show our dislike and bear open testimony against it."

The resolutions were followed by actual resistance in the form of an organization of North Carolina piedmont men known historically as the Regulators, who met the King's army in the Battle of Alamance in 1771. News of that open rebellion spread, and sympathy with the cause of freedom was aroused in other colonies.

In 1772, in the beautiful valley of the Watauga in what is now Tennessee, a group of these rebels formed the first self-governing community in America—the community of Franklin. In his *Winning of the West*, Theodore Roosevelt writes of this Watauga Association:

"It is this fact of the early independence and self-government of the settlers along the headwaters of Tennessee that gives their history its peculiar importance. They were the first men of American birth to establish a free and independent community on the continent."

Occasionally among mountain people you still find someone who claims that his or her ancestor signed the Declaration of Independence. They might very well have signed one of several such documents drawn up throughout those hotheaded mountains. The Watauga Association's declaration of protest against tyranny was written in May, 1772. "Resolved that we do hereby declare ourselves a free and independent people: are, and of a right ought to be, a self-governing association, under the control of no power other than our God and the General Congress; to the maintenance of which we do solemnly pledge to each other our mutual cooperation, our lives, our fortunes, and our most sacred honor."

This was followed by similar resolutions written and signed by indignant citizens at Abington, Virginia, in January, 1775, and Mecklenburg, North Carolina, on May 31, 1775. In that same year the raising of the flag of a new and independent nation in Boonesboro, Kentucky, was celebrated with huge bonfires and Indian war whoops. The leadership taken by our virile Appalachian people underlay the highest reach of the American dream: democracy. And their various written records to that effect asserted the spirit of the ultimate Declaration of Independence adopted in 1776.

By the time Washington was appointed Commander in Chief of the army, the Revolution was already underway in the mountains. The mountain frontiersmen had been guarding the back door of the American colonies, holding the fort against the Indians who were fighting for the British as well as defending their own hunting ground. Such bloody border warfare as the Battle of Point Pleasant in Virginia and the Battle at Boonesboro, Kentucky, mark this earlier period of the Revolution. An American historian, in speaking of the unyielding determination of the Boonesboro men to stand their ground, says: "The feeble little handful of 'rebels' at Boonesboro were true to the last to the principles of the Revolution, and battled as valiantly and suffered as nobly for their freedom and for country as did the men of Bunker Hill or the shivering heroes of Valley Forge."

As the scene shifted to the south, the mountain people had a very definite part in bringing the war to a close.

Cornwallis, on his march to Virginia, sent the men of the mountains a message: If they did not desist from their opposition to British arms, he would march his army over the mountains, hang their leaders, and lay the country waste with fire and sword. Whereupon the mountain men promptly took up fire and sword of their own—in the form of scalping knives and tomahawks and hunting rifles—and delivered their answer personally. They met the Cornwallis army at Kings Mountain. George Washington framed his report of this battle in noble words—he called it "proof of the spiritual resources of the country."

In the mountains you will find the battle remembered in smaller ways. I have seen in a Kentucky shack a little cedar cask which carried water in that battle. From Kentucky comes also the story of the women of a family staying up all night to make gunpowder out of cave saltpeter, redbud ashes, and brimstone, with their vengeance-browed men riding out of the yard yelling, "The Sword of the Lord and of Gideon!" A Tennessee family's hero at the battle dodged into the hollow side of a sycamore and shot through a knothole with a gun named Sweet Lips, for his sweetheart on Back Waters.

In North Carolina there was a man who remembered hearing a joke on Schuyler De Peyster, the royalist officer. As the wild-looking army—in homespun and leather hunting shirts, a balsam sprig or a bucktail stuck jauntily in their coonskin caps, and their long hair flying in the wind—charged the hill, De Peyster heard them give a cheer for liberty. He had heard it before, at Musgrove's Mill, and groaned, "This is that damned yelling set again!" But after the battle was over and the "yelling set" ordered him to dismount while they gave three cheers for liberty, De Peyster thought all hell had broken loose.

A South Forks family has an ancestor who was so seriously wounded in the battle of Kings Mountain that, after the valiant

Commander Ferguson fell, he could not get up to see the corpse
and had to be carried. By the time he saw it, Ferguson, to his
disappointment, had been stripped. It was not a courteous battle.

From Uncle Jake's own neighborhood comes the story of
Benny Wise's wife, who couldn't rest easy in her mind at home
and had followed the army to South Carolina. She waited just
outside Charlotte, in a farmhouse. The day went by, and every
time one of the great big old guns yonder on Kings Mountain
went BOOM! she would cringe and say, "Oh God! Did that one
git Benny?" The last fighting was the worst. Then the mountain
men began thundering down off the hill, shouting and putting
forth some of the best cussing it has ever been permitted a
woman to hear. But Benny Wise's wife wasn't interested, because Benny wasn't one of those who came thundering down off
the hill in the flare of Ferguson's burning wagons.

"Hasn't anybody," she kept asking frantically, and then finally
in dreary breath, "seen Benny Wise?"

At last a smoke-grimed somebody from home came past. "Yes,
I seen him."

"Is he . . . ?" Now that there was someone to tell her, she
could not ask. But the man from home said kindly: "He's hit a
little, but he's all right."

"Oh, thank God!"

"And ain't you heard? We won!"

And Benny Wise's wife could listen then and hear it—hear
the pound of freedom in the hoofs of the victors' horses still thundering past. She did not know it was news that would thrill the
whole country, shock it out of the darkest period of discouragement it had yet known, and give it heart again. All she knew was
that the mountain men had won!

A *Separate* People

*Franky Davis his wife age 87 dide Sep
10 1842 she had nerve fite wolves all
nite at shogar camp to save her caff
throde fire chunks to save caff the camp
war haf mile from home now she must
have nerve to fite wolf all nite.*

"IT took a brave woman to leave England behind,"
a mountain man once said thoughtfully. "A still braver one after
the boat had landed to follow the rivers on inland, and when the
rivers stopped, it took the bravest ones yet to come on up into the
hills."

When you walk in the hills, even the mildest of them, it is an
ever-recurrent surprise to find that within half an hour from the
main highway you can be out of sight and sound of anything
civilized. Following a little creek, your whole preoccupation be-
comes a wonder at the variation of tone in the crystal-clear
stream; at the high dry sound of fall in the trees overhead if it's
coming on toward that time of year; or the separate sharpness of
the first snow to hit. And every now and then you think of those
woods when they were really wilderness.

The quiet then was an awesome silence, broken not by small
reliefs from mechanization, but by the scream of the panther—
the long, piercing, quivering, half-human wail that people who
have heard it say seems to come from nowhere and yet be everywhere. Such a sound must have frozen the pioneer woman in her
tracks with horror, and sent her faint for an instant with dread of
the wilderness still ahead of her. Even more than the sounds of
the wilderness, the women dreaded those other times when there

was a suspicious lack of sound—the sign that Indians were about. Those were the times when the men told their women to keep their eyes and ears open and their mouths shut. Those were the times when the men left the women to go ahead, telling them if they heard a shot to get behind a tree and wait.

A salty West Virginian, who is a "dear lover of antiquity" and takes great pains to dig up everything he can concerning his forerunners, told me with a chuckle that one of the womenfolk in his history once got behind the wrong tree. An Indian grabbed her. But she was husky—she had some fight in her and got away. She was the only one of the family who did. But he said she was a woman with life, and at their last family reunion there were enough of her descendants to cover an acre standing solid.

The woman of the wilderness, though wolf packs howled and wildcats screamed and every tree shadow held the lurking fear of Indians, did not turn back. She went on, because her man was being driven by some spirit of search and she was staying by him.

The daring of those early days of search is still there. It is in that unwieldy long-barreled rifle hanging over the fireplace, with the old shot pouch and powder horn beside it. That rifle brought the first woman of the household safely through the wilderness, to the particular high piece of globe her man had decided he wanted to be his.

The homing note of those days is still there too. It is in the clumsy old looms that sometimes are still found taking up too much of the small house back off the road, although more usually they will be found moved down into the community weaving room set up by the local school to keep the time-old arts alive.

The daring and the homing, they are still there. They are in the well-set head and steadfast eyes of the best of the young mountain women. The spirit of the girl who came into the mountains—strong, lithe, vivacious, daring anything at the side of her chosen man, a border chieftain—still lives in the free, sure swing of the mountain girl's walk.

And there is something magnificent about the old mountain woman—in the patience and endurance in the thin set of her mouth, the friendly interest in all pleasant things at the wrinkled corners of her eyes. It is a saneness amounting to serenity, letting her wait the end of age calm in the knowing that while her kind may not have found all they set out to find, they have found a place to search.

The mountain-frontiersman felt that if he had a strong right arm, an ax, and a gun, the world was his to conquer. The trash-lazy mountaineer is his exceptional descendant. True, mountain men are inclined to chafe at the tedium of routine that offers no individual challenge. Plugging along steadily at a job for the sole purpose of getting enough money ahead to be able to quit some-day does not appeal to their sense of reason. It seems to them much more sensible to work when there is work to be done, but when a right day comes along to go hunting, or to share enthusiastically a favorite cliff with a visiting friend, enjoy it. Why strive frantically toward something ahead when you can have it as you go along?

They may take a serious interest in doing well whatever is their job, and if they think you are interested, they courteously will share that too. Yet they speak of their work almost offhandedly, as though of an incident in their days, on the way through. Their very air and mien, those with pride of race wrought into the fiber, seem to cancel out the idea of work being man's ever-after punishment for his fall from grace. Apparently mountain men have never heard that man *had* fallen from grace.

It has frequently been said that what applies to Appalachian life far up the creek, or in some lost "shut-in," is a far call from that of rich farmland along the river bottoms. The little town of Moorefield, nestled along the South Branch of the Potomac, with the mountains rising up on either side keeping their distance, has obviously long known the economic advantages of riverside fields where the green corn grows high. Yet when I ventured to an old-time resident that they really could not call themselves mountain people, could they, he looked me pleasantly in the eye and said firmly, "We like to think we are." And indeed there was rationale in his considered, direct assertion.

In many respects the leisurely valley town with its sidewalk bench under a spreading tree congenially located at the hub—near the Old Stone Tavern, 1780—is characteristic of a way of life brought into the wilderness by that virile race of colonists. Not far from the one stop light is the Fort Pleasant Meeting House. Built along a tree-shaded lane, for over a hundred years it served both as church and schoolhouse.

And the town's names read like a roster of the several European peoples melded into a distinctive entity by the same lodestar that drew them to a new land: liberty. Bean, Harper, Spencer, Allen, Friddle, Duffey, Harminson, Kuykendall, Hawse, Pawnall, and Bayliss are a conglomerate representation.

You are unlikely to find such evidence of stage-coach travel as old stone taverns in the more remote mountain communities. Yet there, even more, it is like stepping outside "these giddy-paced times" for a while. And all through the rocky and forested Appalachian range, you can still find names resounding of an American Revolution roll call: Bryan, Fitzgerald, Daniels, Shafer, Ristau, Davenport, Hildebrand, Vance, McGuilkin, Stevens, McGraw, and Clark.

For the most part Anglo-Saxon in background, they too had set out to find freedom. And that first pioneer man and woman, climbing up into a high place where the mighty loops of the hills made a hallelujah garland around the sky, could not foresee that the clock of time would stop for them there.

They did not foresee that the hallelujah garland would become a potent barrier, shutting off their descendants from the rest of the world; shaping their political and economic and social lives along entirely different patterns from their compatriots in the out and beyond.

There were no maps to show them they had chosen a place without waterways to make natural routes of communication. They knew that the roads they had followed, or made themselves, into the mountains were bad. But at the time of those early migrations all roads were bad, and mountain passes not much worse than others.

They could not know that for the next hundred and fifty years their roads and their pioneer way of life would change so little that they would become a separate people, set apart from all others by virtue of custom, character, dialect, and by certain physical and mental traits they had brought into the wilderness with them, which their long isolation there would intensify.

Shakespeare's America

Margit Carpenter age 87 1875 dide jun
5 ware good womin good to the pore
when she ware amind.

AS a race, the people of our southern mountains
speak softly. Even their most commonplace remarks somehow
are made to sound secret, and of greatest importance. The
women especially speak softly, their voices often plaintively
sweet, pitched in a minor key and lilting upward, so that the last
word of every sentence is almost sung.

Their phrasing has a rhythm to it, such as "all her days,"
meaning a lifetime. Then there are: times I recall when; if happen you pass; enduring the time; the day long; over the ridge and
down; I wonder me if; far lands across; the green shadder gum
tree; whar all to?

Sometimes it is an arbitrary accent on the single word that
gives the rhythmic effect, as: "agreement, hostile"—the accent
placed on whichever part of the word strikes their sense of
sound, then the whole stretched out drawlingly to its full length.

They have an instinctive knack with words, somehow bringing out of a limited and ancient vocabulary a wealth of rich
idiom. Shapes of phrases repeat themselves and the same sounds
re-echo, giving, oddly enough, vividness rather than monotony—
as in their use of double words: down-log; sulphur-match; man-
person; flower-thing; mother-woman; storm of rain; tooth-dentist;
neighbor-people; ocean-sea; ham-meat; cookin'-pan; belly-empty;
biscuit-bread; rifle-gun; ridin'-critter; cow-brute; preacher-man;
granny-woman, we-uns; chanty-song.

Adjectives and adverbs are used as though they had plenty of them. "I thought shorely undoubtedly of a sartin hit war so," you will hear, perhaps of a rumor believed in and found in relief not to be true. Or the wondering comment on a girl very slight in stature may be, "She's a peart little thing, got plenty of sense, but the least spindlingest little old thing."

Negatives especially mount up: That boy never done nothin' nohow; I hain't got nary none; I can't get no rest nohow; I never seen no man of no kind do no washin'.

Since the southern mountain people have lived to themselves, a race apart for almost two centuries, their idiom has come to be curiously intense—drawn from their own experiences and kept fresh in that it is always firsthand. An independent and individualistic people about everything else, it is natural that they should be so in speech too. Thus, when it suits them to use nouns for verbs, they do—and very effectively: I didn't fault him for hit; that b'ar'll meet me for a month; chair bottomin' is easy settin' down work; who'll funeralize the corpse?; are you a-fixin' to go squirrelin'?; he hain't much on sweetheartin'; I don't confidence them dogs; that creek turkey-tails out into numerous little forks.

In the same way, if a verb feels better to them as a noun, that's the way they use it: You can git you one more gittin' of wood out of that pile; I didn't hyear no give-out about hit; listen, all you settin' rounders!

The same freedom goes for the way adjectives get put into action: Hit grumbled the old woman some; he was biggin' and biggin' the story; he went lick-splittin' hit down the road; much [make much over] that dog and see won't he come; come toeteeterin' in; I didn't do nary a thing to contrary her; hit benasties a man's mind.

And with even more fanciful flux, verbs flow into adjectives: the travelin'est hosses; the talkin'est woman; the workin'est man; the nothin'-doin'dest day; she war just a little set-along child; Jim's the disablest one of the family; hit's a fotched-on hat.

Adverbs, too, get their twist: A person has a rather about whar he'll be buried; I hope yore folks are all gaily.

Southern mountain speech, which is peculiarly pleasing when

1   The mountains rise like a misty dream of greatness.

2 The river was called Wild Run only
because of the nature of the people.

it is heard, is apt to look crude when it is put down in print. In actuality, however, far from being a rude dialect, much of it springs from the classics. Many expressions are Biblical. They use "generation" to mean a certain breed of people, just as Moses did when he bemoaned the corrupted children of God as "a perverse and crooked generation."

In the main, most of the idiom is a direct carry-over of old English. Queen Elizabeth herself used their "begone! have done with! a sorry fellow; a fere and fellowy man." Out of Chaucer comes their term "feisty," meaning impertinent; "fray" for fight; "gorm" for muss; "pack" for carry. "Mast" is an ancient word for game herbage and can be heard in the comment of any present-day hunter. The mountain wedding festivities, called the "infare," came from the old prenuptial celebration of the bride-groom. And right out of Shakespeare one of my fifth-grade students in a North Carolina mountain school reported that some-body in the back of the room was acting the fool by saying, "He's wearin' the bells!"

The lack of gap between Shakespearean times and ours can sometimes be linguistically startling, as when you hear the term "cuckold" used as familiarly as though it were Othello himself moaning, "That cuckold lives in bliss." Women borrow a "tod-dick" of wool, as they did in *The Winter's Tale*. The past of "helped," which is said as "holp," has justification in *King John* when Philip is questioning his legitimacy by declaring, "Sir Rob-ert never holp make this leg. . . ."

From the same redoubtable source comes "anticky; harry; misdoubt; rift"; "stout," meaning healthy; "childing" meaning to be pregnant; "lay," to wager.

They say "fur" with Sir Philip Sidney, and "furder" with Lord Bacon. They carry a "handkercher"; see a "sighte" of flowers or "beastes"; "cavil," argue—as did the characters of *Canterbury Tales*. "Peart; afore; amind; sech; yander," all are good Elizabe-than words.

"Ary" and "nary" are merely convenient contractions from the classical "e'er a," and "ne'er a." The universal use of "hit" for "it" springs from a time before true English itself, being the Anglo-

Saxon neuter of "he." And if the fireside and store-front remark in the mountains is sometimes rough, sometimes definitely beyond the pale of polite conversation, so was the fireside conversation of Queen Elizabeth!

The language of the southern mountains, as all etymologists agree, is far more survival than degeneration. However, its particular flavor comes from the curious combination of a manner of speech centuries old and of honorable origin with terms that are rankly out of a raw new country, "Yan side," they twang out, and use strong past tenses like "blowed" and "growed."

Their mispronunciations are lusty: "char, b'ar." Sturdy use is made of that "r," often as a substitute for the final "s" in "was." Furthermore, they mispronounce at will. "Whar is hit?" someone will ask, and then discover, "Thar hit is." Someone else may choose to rhyme it another way. "Whur is hit? Thur hit is." There is no romantic trace back to ancient terminology in their mispronunciations. They merely mispronounce in whatever way is at hand.

And although the woman of the house may be singing some song whose origin is to be found in the Percy *Reliques*—and singing it as Chaucer mentions it being sung, "entuned in her nose full sweetly"—still, there certainly is nothing classical about the "shucky beans" and "sow belly" and "sass" she is fixing for supper. That is "p'int blank" out of the hills.

So are their place names. Mountain place names can be vividly descriptive but they are obviously inventions of right around home: Squabble Creek; Morning Star; Pigeon Roost; Troublesome; Wind Ridge; Stand Around; Thousand Sticks; Mud Fork; Cranberry; Sally's Back Bone; Pole Cat Holler; Hell for Sartin.

Both the survival and the earthy freshness of the mountain speech, however, have had their origin and reason in the peculiar separation that the high lengths of hills have made between mountain people and the world. Now, as modern developments change this, it is only to be expected that survival and freshness both will be lost in ordinariness. Yet it is apt to go slowly, that combination of the very old and the very new, because the minor quality is somehow an air the mountain people have inherited from their whole history.

The old ballads should go too; should have been lost years ago in the blare of radio and jukeboxes, and again now in the popularity of TV. Yet you find the old ballads still being clung to and sung occasionally—for a reason Shakespeare knew:

> That old and antique song we heard last night;
> Methought it did relieve my passion much,
> More than light airs and recollected terms
> Of these most brisk and giddy-paced times.

So, in a tin-front restaurant of a mountain town growing quickly ordinary to meet the sudden trade going past on the broad new highway, you still can hear a mountain boy, half in jest, half wryly, make a kind of pristine song of the news, "My gal's quit me. I'm about to lock my heart and throw the key away."

Sins of the Flesh

Charley Kiney age 72 ma[y] 10 1852
war farmer liv in N.C. on blue rige at
Kiney Gapp he had 4 womin cors marid
to won rest live on farm all went to field
work to mak gran all went to crib for the
bred all went to smoke house for ther
mete he cild bout 75 to 80 hogs ever yere
and womin never had words bout his
havin so many womin [if it] wod be this
time thar wod be hare puld they raz 42
children belong to him all wen to prechin
together nothin sed they des everibodi
go long smoth with won nother he
made brandy all of his lif never had any
foes got long smoth with everibodi i nod
him

EVERY man—the head of his own house, the law in his own hollow—lived his own life. But when a man carried that independent way of life to the lengths that Charley Kiney did, he became a character. And although the wild lavishness of Charley Kiney's particular patriarchy was unusual, every mountain state has had in it some man of like stature whose progeny spread out over several counties and came to be counted on to carry the vote for that section. The others maintained several separate establishments. But Charley Kiney is the only such potentate within my knowledge who so blandly attempted—and evidently succeeded—in carrying it off all under one roof.

Irregular unions, on a much lesser scale, were not uncommon all through the mountains and might occur anywhere along the social ladder. There was the youngish woman who did the local wash in one mountain community and took things comfortably as they came. She had a likable, bony face with a healthy curve to it. All her children were healthy too. There were three of them. She kept the two eldest dressed in their respective fathers' old clothes, cut down, and they bore their respective fathers' names. But she was uncertain about what to name the new one, and sincerely troubled.

"I prayed all night the night hit come," she said earnestly, "tryin' to think who hit's pappy is—because if thar's one thing I'm particular about, hit's my honor!"

Going on up the scale, the attitude tightens. The better people do not condone such laxness by any means. Still, should the misfortune occur, they feel the condemnation should fall on the parents and not on the child. That the child have a fair chance, therefore, it takes a place without stigma in the household, along with the children born into the family rightfully.

In the days of mountain life when creek beds were the only roads there were, which was not so long ago, sometimes it might be months or even years before the preacher got into remote districts, and marital strictures necessarily slackened. A state of marriage was often declared by an enamored young couple merely moving into a house of their own farther up the creek.

But the general lack of social shock accompanying illegitimacy goes far back. It was not unknown among their forebears. Irregular unions, in fact, were so common in the Old Country, they were recognized by law. An old English map shows widely spreading properties as belonging—quite simply, in unashamed type at the top—to "William, Bastard Duke of Normandy." Even the Irish St. Brigit was born out of wedlock. And certainly the sins of the flesh, amiable frailties of mankind since time began, have not bypassed the southern mountains, often called "Shakespeare's America."

Logs by 100

*Joef Pyatt Jan 15 dide 1864 he war
farmer made logs by 100*

LIKELY he needed to make "logs by 100." There was, first of all, shelter to consider. Those logs were hacked out with patient sure blows of the ax and then scribed at the corners so they could fit neatly when the neighbors came to help raise the sides of the new house and were paid in roast venison and a jollification afterward.

There were the great puncheons to be hewn for the floor boards—leaving a few of them loose so the wife-woman could store her preserves and pickles and jars of wild huckleberries and gooseberries underneath.

There were boards to be split for shingles, split with a froe from straight-grained oak. You still can find some of them occasionally, twice the size and length of our shingles now and grown gray with the years of moss between them. A man had to be careful to lay these shingles in the increase of the moon, or they would cup. Sometimes a low shingle was left loose, to have handy to reach up and get if a "youngin' was just a-hurtin' for a lickin'."

Next there was the mantelpiece—the fireboard; often half a sourwood log, the deeply serrated bark setting off the stone fireplace well.

The solid oak door had to be made so it could be left open for air unless a man wanted to bar it against someone he didn't want to see. A mountain man likes air. Most of these old houses, they will tell you, had cracks you could put the cat through. Even standing in the middle of the room you had to hang on to your hat, it was so drafty. And when a real "windin'" spell struck, you had to put rocks on the bedcovers to keep them from sailing out the cracks and into the next county. Rain came in one side of the house and went out the other. And many a morning you would wake up with your breath frozen on the coverlid.

Even a present-day guest of the old-type mountain homes can attest to their particular variety of air conditioning. One man who went hunting in the southern part of West Virginia tells about the house in which he stayed. It was so far modernized as to have a thermometer. He said when he woke up in the morning the thermometer registered eighteen above inside the house. When he tried it outside, it rose to twenty. So he went outdoors and got dressed.

After the early frontiersman had built his house, there was its furnishing to consider. It was found that hickory was good for chair frames, but white oak was best to split for the seats. A chair seat made of white oak will "wear a pair of britches out settin' on hit afore the chair seat goes." There were the beds and a table and a cupboard to be fashioned and enduringly put together with maple pegs. There was the little rhododendron root table—for "the Bible to set on." Some of this old furniture is beautiful, with the original pale virginity of the pine wood turning slowly golden, and cherry deepening with the years.

Every self-respecting man made his wife a quilting frame, and there was the dough bowl to hollow out; the red cedar "piggin," with a "hand holt" at the side, to carry water from the spring. There was the broom to make—splitting a white-oak stick into ribbons, tying one end of them, then spreading them. There were the gourds to hollow out for the soft soap, and for the grease to keep the leather door hinges from squeaking.

There were the wooden lasts to be made for the family's shoes —although of course only one last was needed for each person. One last did for both feet. There were no rights and lefts to those homemade brogans, square cut from tanned hide. At night the shoe that was to go on the right foot was put where the right foot would step into it in the morning, and the left one was put handy to the left foot, and gradually they wore to shape.

Shoes, however, were something the mountain people could take or leave. One woman told me she had never had a pair of shoes until she was nineteen. "And then," she remembered merrily, "the first pair I did put on my feet cotched me and throwed me." A man told me that he wore out his first pair of shoes from the inside, his feet were so toughened. Some of the old people still resent shoes. "These derned contraptions for the feet that'll make four-toed creatures of mankind yet!" stormed an irate oldster of a pair that were hurting.

Now that he had his homefolks fixed out, the mountain man had to provide shelter for his stock, although mountain barns are very makeshift affairs. But there was the apple house to put up, and beehives to make; and the sled to contrive, for often the trail to his house was too tortuous, or the creek too tempestuous, for a wagon to travel. The sleds are still simply two oak runners curved at the front end with a frame riding them, and a single tree to hitch the horse to. There were the hoe handles to make, cutting each one to the proper size of each member of the family —for everyone took a row, from the "granny-woman" down to the littlest "set-along child." When a piece of especially good bird's-eye maple or ash was found, it was laid aside to replace the stock of a gun, come the next rainy day.

When somebody died, one of the neighbors knocked together a coffin. Once this kindly service was a little previous. Les Alden got "bad off sick" and someone of the family sent for the coffin-maker. The man came, and went right out to the shed and started hammering. He didn't bother to come in and measure, because everybody knew that Les was the longest Alden of the name. But Les, hearing the racket, asked what it was. When he was told, he raised up on his elbow and hollered furiously out toward the shed, "Quit that! I hain't dead yet!"

The man who had come to make the coffin got mad too. He

had walked a long way. "Well, don't send for me next time till you need me!"

The gabled old house on yon side a winding stream and just this side a mountain, yet with enough bottom land in front of it for haystacks to drowse peacefully in the twilight; the high, narrow old house with double porches, the one upstairs latticed in the old southern style and used as a plunder room, the downstairs one sociable with low-legged homemade chairs; the old log cabins, bespeaking the sturdiness of those builders first to come into the wilderness; even the little plank house built into the side of a mountain, its unpainted sides making one with the wooded heights behind it, with the very smoke from its squat stone chimney drifting out to become a part of the tender distances—all these houses have a quality no others in America quite have. It is a quality that comes of everything about them having been put there by the hearts and heads and hands of the people living in them, and all from material at hand.

Something of that completeness goes into their particular quality of hospitality. Their independence lets them be gracious. There is no more heart-warming greeting in the world than "Heigh-ho, I'm God-proud to see you." Nor is there a much better farewell than "Come back. . . ."

"Come stay all night" is a familiar and cordial byword. If it's a warm day, you are invited to "draw up a chair and cool off." If the day is cold, they urge you to put off your parting with, "Best linger up by the fire. That air's stirrin' cool." If their invitation to share a meal with them has an apologetic cast, the apology is purely verbal. "Our food hain't much, but reach out and take yore needs." The obvious feeling lying behind the prelude is that what is good enough for them is good enough for you.

The natural bearing, as a whole, of the highlander suggests indeed that he is as good as you are, and maybe somewhat better. It is not an arrogant attitude, and certainly not defensive. It is merely a calm assurance of equality that goes deeper than pride or thought. It allows the highland people to make that calm scrutiny of the outsider which sometimes irritates the outlander and sometimes is badly mistaken for stupidity. They are not gaping.

They merely are taking your measure. If they "confidence" you, their hospitality is very genuine, and often is offered with a generous dignity that leaves you feeling honored.

I have seen that feeling written in cross-stitch on an old-fashioned sampler hanging on the wall of a rustic dwelling high in the Carolina mountains. The sampler hung at the broad turn of the stairs, only a few steps up, but there was height in its cross-stitched words, and warming depth: "Joy be with you while you stay, and peace go with you on your way."

On the other hand, the proffered hospitality may be of the sort you hesitate to accept. Once I fell in the creek and landed in such a predicament. An angular Amazon who lived up that way happened along and fished me out from where I'd fallen in the water trying to get over a high rail fence beside it.

She had been to the store and had put on a hat for the journey. Even in my dripping condition I looked at her and thought to myself that it took more than strength to put on a hat. But she was kind. She insisted on my going into her house and drying off and having a glass of buttermilk. The glass she picked up off the cluttered table was frosted by intimate and unwashed use. I said thank you, but I really didn't care for any buttermilk. She said pre-emptorily that buttermilk was good for folks. But I didn't have to have any after all, because when she went to get the buttermilk, which was in the dishpan, she found that while she had been at the store her oldest daughter had thought it was dishwater and pitched it out the door. Whereupon the annoyed woman picked up the dishpan and whacked the girl over the head with it.

"Ahem," said a disheveled man appearing in the doorway of the other room. Evidently he had dozed off and just been awakened by the racket. "But hain't that thunder?"

"No hit hain't," said the woman shortly. "That was me, a-bangin' on Clarissa. She throwed out the buttermilk and I was a-lookin' to give the company some."

The man scratched his thin hair interestedly. "God-burn certain," he said, "I thought shore that was thunder."

While the social system of the mountains certainly is not

stuffy, it has its definite scale. It hits its high and low there as well as anywhere else. The meal you are invited to share at the opposite pole from buttermilk may be served in a big old dining room with the table groaning like the proverbial festive board, and the sideboard loaded with pies and cakes and preserved peaches, all prepared from a kitchen with the floor "so clean you could eat off of it."

I remember breakfasts especially in a modern mountain house. (Modern mountain houses, like many things about the modernization of our forgotten people, keep the best of what is natural to the locality. The better ones being built now are made of river stone and bark shingles.)

I remember that the shingles of this particular house were the same gray as the oak-tree trunk outside the window. I remember the freshness of the strawberries from the garden, and the sweetness of the clean homespun table mats and napkins on the handmade table. I remember the way the early sun flooded the breakfast room, and the grace that began the day. There was life to that grace, as though each day were a fresh beginning, full of infinite possibilities and adventure. The grace was for guidance, for wisdom, given with such lift to it that one expected wonderful things of that day and so, expecting and looking for them, they came, one way or another.

In the fertile bottom lands there are great houses as well. The whole stretch of the South Potomac Valley that wanders around eastern West Virginia—from Moorefield, through historic Petersburg and Romney, scourged by both sides during the Civil War, on to Franklin at the edge of Virginia—is dignified with fine old homesteads. Much of that farmland was surveyed by George Washington for Lord Fairfax. Despite the ravages of war, there are still vestiges of pioneer prosperity: hand-blocked wallpaper imported from France depicting hunting scenes, cherry-paneled dining rooms, gabled barns and decorative fences.

Back in the mile after mile of forested mountains bounding the Valley are also landmarks of early hardship and privation, such as the log cabin in which Lincoln's mother was born. Wherever possible, that log beginning has been carefully preserved in the pillared and winged houses, through which visitors are graciously shown by fifth- or sixth-generation owners.

"Logs by 100," to make the houses that symbolize the strength and simplicity of a race of virile and hospitable people.

A French Creek Horse Trade

Alan Dilinger age 86 dide jun 1 1889
ware grate trader

SOUTHERN mountain people are born traders, and often they give the knack a little extra fillip. A famous horse trader in the French Creek district in West Virginia had the fashion of justifying all his particular deals with a quotation from Scripture.

Once he found himself stuck with a horse with the heaves. All the neighbors knew the animal's condition and refused even to dicker. On Court Day, he took it into the county seat, and although it changed hands seven times in the course of a day, he came home that night with the selfsame nag on his hands. He was sitting on the fence looking at it the next morning, feeling low in his mind, when a stranger came by. They got to talking and, while discussing the weather, it developed that the man was an itinerant preacher. He was making his rounds on foot and a long road lay ahead of him.

The horse trader brightened.

His wife, coming to the door a while later to call him in to dinner, found him standing with his hands in his pockets, contentedly whistling a little through his teeth. He was looking down the road where a horse and rider seemed to be just making it around the hemlocks of the next bend. His wife shaded her eyes with her hand, to be sure.

"That ain't that ridin'-critter of yo'rn with the heaves a-goin' yonder, is hit?"

He admitted modestly that it was.

"You didn't git anything for hit, did you?"

On the contrary, he had made a right good deal.

"Good la," she exclaimed, "who on earth would give you anything for that old nag?"

"Some preacher."

His wife stared at him. "A preacher! Why, however in the world could you do a thing like that?"

She was so honestly indignant that he studied on it. Then he said, "He was a stranger and I tuk him in."

Of Blue and Fine Linen

Lily Wiseman age 82 dide feb 23 1875
Spon & wove cloth made all they wore

"And all the women that were wise
hearted did spin with their hands,
and brought that which they had spun,
both of blue, and of purple, and of scarlet,
and of fine linen."
—Exodus 35:25

THE women of Exodus were spinners, and so are our southern mountain women. It is a heritage that goes back through hundreds of generations.

In its Appalachian beginning, the whole process had a timeless measure to it. Standing barefoot in a cool stream washing the wool, then spreading it on the sunny grass to dry, were tasks that had the width and ease of the whole outdoors. And when the wheel and spindle her man had made was brought outdoors so the spinner could stand under the idle sky of summer while she spun, the natural pull and flow in the movement of spinning became part of a bigger pull and flow.

And a woman could take her satisfaction in color at such work, dipping the skeins she had spun into the dyes and their variants of her own devising.

With all the excitement of discovery, she found that the red root of the vining madder plants, with their small yellow flowers and berries, could be boiled into a dye the tonal quality of which ranged from madder pink to scarlet or crimson. Then there was tomato green, brown from black-walnut hulls, yellow from hickory bark. Indigo blue was another favorite color, for it too summoned her ingenuity. Its base was yielded from the wild pea plant with trailing vine and lacy white flowers. Indigo could be dyed the tender blue of a sleepy child's eyes, or to the depth of winter sky at twilight.

If a pack peddler got up her way, which was seldom, or if her man journeyed down off the mountain to a settlement on Court Day, he might think to fetch her a package of commercial indigo, and alum to set her dyes. Otherwise, the commonest form of potash alum—wood ashes—served very well as a fixative.

With all her materials in order, at the loom she could combine her pretties as she had a mind to.

The thud and clack of the loom marked off something more than an art impulse. It gave the woman's hands something to do while she thought. Or if she had thought too much—about the uncertainties, or about how so many of her plans had gone awry —then there was something wonderful in seeing a thing take shape under her hands and stay that way. And in weaving, if she made a mistake, she could undo it.

The old hand-loomed coverlets had life running through them: Log Cabin, Castle City, Blooming Leaf, Martha Washington, Pine Bloom, Spider Web, Young Man's Fancy, and Rose in the Wilderness.

Often it was the more utilitarian stuff for shirts and pants she was weaving. And that brought a satisfaction of a different sort. The men thought a good deal of homespun flax cloth. "Them britches war rough on a feller's hide. But they'd last a man. They warn't like these boughten pants made so thin you've got to be careful how you walk." If the men bothered with socks at all, they were knitted from homespun wool.

As the mountains grew more populous, "fotched on" calico from the out and beyond afforded another outlet for a woman's creative urge. Then she could ride horseback or carry her wares on foot to the crossroads store. There she could trade her eggs and goose feathers—nothing so downy for her as a goose-feather bed—for spool thread, and ready-made cloth with all the colors there were!

From calico scraps and pieces the women cut out their own designs, which later would be arranged into a quilted pattern. Roses, Lilies, Sunflowers, Jacob's Ladder, Sun and Moon, Maple Leaf, Faith and Fortune, Lee's Surrender, and again Log Cabin —and once more the truth of life was in the store-bought material.

Quilting bees, when the neighborhood women got chattily together for the day to help one another stitch their patterns onto a plain white background, were the club meetings of the mountains. It was the menfolk, who came in for the traditional chicken-pie supper, however, who invented the quilt courting game.

They called it "cat shakin'"—and poor cat! A quilt was spread out on the floor; all the courting-age young bent down, took firm hold of its edges with both hands, and raised up slowly with it. Then the cat was thrown in and the boys tried to shake it out toward their best girl. That was the idea of the game; whichever girl the wild-eyed tabby leaped nearest to would marry first. The shakers laughed and yelled as they tossed the oracle of their fate from one to another, and high in the air. It was only a game, leaving the night's chosen one flushed and chattering nonsense to the boy whose strong flick of a wrist had sent the cat her way, and who scarcely could listen for watching her.

Log rollings by the men for a neighbor's new house were occasions for quilting bees too, as were sugar parties. These were early spring affairs, when a family invited the countryside in to help boil down into sugar the sweet water they'd collected from maple trees—but not all of it. When the syrup reached the taffy stage, the big-eyed children were each given a little dish of it to roll into candy balls. And where the young were, there was courting.

An eggshell blown empty through a small hole at each end and carefully filled with the still-liquid sugar "made as nice an Easter egg present as a girl would ever care to get," said a woman who didn't need to remember that excitement is half your

own excitement—she was still a merry one. Or you could mold
the hardening sugar into the shape of a heart and slip it to your
true love when nobody was noticing, sitting as they were around
the evening fire telling riddles.

Or the yearning young might both be so shy they would wait
till the "play-party games," danced to the music of fiddlers who
stroked and teased and whanged their instruments till the stars
rang, were over. They would wait till he was walking her home
in the half-dark, half-light hours that might be nearing morning,
a dawning of the elemental rightness of deep content, known and
acknowledged. There was no sense of time moving too fast, or
closing in, although it was doing both. But the peace of the night
of the sugar heart would not ever be hurried away.

A cherished quilt fragment I saw had something of that tenuous essence. The owner said her grandmother, whose pattern it
was, had been so choice of that quilt it had never touched water.
She didn't know whatever had happened to the whole of it, but
the rescued sample the spry little graying lady showed me was in
safekeeping now. It was hanging on the wall, in a mellowed old
maple picture frame. The oval shape of the frame echoed the
opening petals of pink and white roses, blooming on a curving
green branch.

The elemental quality of those early mountains coverlets,
made by hand from necessity and with the hardness of the life
running through them gentled by beauty-hunger, can never
quite be recaptured. Yet the indifferent years between are now
bringing increase to their value. Not only do mountain schools
keep the early arts alive in their elective courses, but that heritage is being actively fostered all through the southern highlands.
Farm women are practicing the art of weaving—not britches, of
course, nor do they make their own dyes. Even so, no Appalachian Fair or Festival would be complete without an Old Time
Crafts exhibit: colorful quilts, wood carving, pottery, hand-
loomed rugs and table mats.

And not so long ago I watched a mountain woman spinning.
She was spinning wool for her husband's hunting socks. He
proudly displayed the pair he had on, which she already had

made for him. But she thought the new ones would be better—the thread wouldn't be so bumpy. She was just learning to spin. She made a very pleasant picture, a young woman whose main sense was poise as she stood by the wheel in the fall of lamplight.

Lure of the Hunt

Soonzy Ollis age 84 dide June 10 1871
grates bar honter & turkies bee trees by
honders and ratel snak by 100 cild deer
by thousand I no him well

EVER since Daniel Boone got Kentucky settled with his fabulous tales of the game there and led the way to it by joining buffalo trails into a road, the southern mountains have been happy hunting grounds. And surprisingly, the diversity of the hunt there is not much different today than it was in the early days of our country when those first bold spirits broke the bondage of routine, oppression, banalities, or things they wanted to forget, to set forth for the free life of the wilds.

There is an old account of one Sam Pringle's adventure with a bear near Tygart's River, in what was then the Virginia of 1846, that could nearly double for a similar encounter in North Carolina a few years ago.

"Sam Pringle," so goes the account, "was no coward, but the huge size of the beast loomed so formidably that even the intrepid hunter felt a sensibility akin to fear come over him. He realized that he was alone in that boundless wilderness, within twenty paces of a beast of crushing strength. Should his shot fail to reach a vital spot, he well knew the infuriated monster might charge—that it would be a hand-to-hand fight with knife and tomahawk pitted against gnashing fangs and ripping claws. . . ."

It goes on tensely to tell about a mighty avalanche of claws, bare fangs, and iron muscle, with bloody froth dripping in ropy strings from spiked jaws.

The present-day "intrepid hunter" is a mountain man by choice, having arrived at that by way of what Robert Louis Stevenson termed for himself "The 'Circle' "—the "advancement from complexity to simplicity." In the more recent North Carolina encounter, if the bear was not exactly monster, it was, according to admiring observers, "too big to stand under." The excitement about Sam Brown's brush with a bear had been spread by the observers, the hunter himself not being inclined to dramatize, although the whole drama of these present-day stories lies in that very ease, along with a quiet humor. But sitting around a picnic fire one night, the picnickers finally prevailed upon Sam to tell about it.

The stars were very near that night, and red sparks flew to heaven from the whole balsam tree somebody had chopped down and kept feeding to the fire. The fire was in a kind of balsam valley almost at the top of a mountain, between two peaks blacker than the sky. One rose as though the flat of a hand had made a gesture upward with one superb movement. The other peak was cragged and cut. All down around and below us the wind in the hemlocks was a wild, mad thing. But it was very quiet where we were. Even so, we had to listen to hear, the story was told so casually.

"One particularly mean bear had been getting the dogs, so we set off after her. I saw her once up the branch, but my gun jammed. It had done that once before and I'd knocked it against a stump. So I tried it again. But this time I broke it. So I left it at the stump and ran on.

"I met the bear at a sharp turn and we stood there looking at each other. She looked like she couldn't make up her mind what to do, but mine was already made up. I turned around and ran. I looked for a club to hit her with, but by the time I'd found one, she'd loped off in the other direction.

"The next time I caught up with her, I was up on a bluff and she was down a ways, leaping on a favorite dog of mine. She had it in her paws, and would hold it and fall on it. That made me mad. I got excited and started down toward her, throwing rocks at her as I ran. I hit her, but I didn't do any good. Then I remembered a knife I had in my pocket, and I jumped on her and started to hack. I could feel the knife cut, but I didn't seem to hurt her. Then I realized I was cutting on her ribs and moved over.

"The bear was mad too, and we rolled downhill together. I had her about cleaned by the time we hit bottom, but still she wouldn't die. Doggonedest bear to die I ever saw. I looked up and saw Bert Aldridge aiming at it—or me, one or the other, I couldn't be sure, he was so excited. But I was glad to see him. I yelled, 'Bert, shoot this bear—only come down here and do it.' "

Once caught by the fascination of bear hunting, everything else is put second. Whenever the right kind of day comes along to carry scent, any other occupation or interest is dropped promptly to train bear dogs. Whole intent days are spent dragging a piece of bearhide, tied to the rear bumper of a car, over the country with the dog pack in tow, teaching them the scent.

Even politics are forgotten. They tell the story in eastern Tennessee about the time the Governor got up that way. The local politicians, by way of cottoning up to the mighty man, produced their best for him—a bear hunt. But they grew so interested in listening to their own particular dogs giving tongue out over the hills and valleys that they forgot about its being the Governor's party. Suddenly one of them took a whiff of the midnight supper they had intended. Then he drawled, "How do you like yore meat, Gov'nor?"

"A little burned," sniffed the Governor obligingly.

"Wal, she's a-burnin'," sang back the hunter cheerfully.

Almost anywhere in the mountains you can hear bear stories. In Avery County in North Carolina, they talk about Spenser Shooks's traps. He contrived very ingenious ones. He contrived one so ingenious he got caught in it himself. Fortunately he happened to have a hand hatchet with him and hacked himself out. It took him three days.

Once War Clark told me, comfortably from his old age on the front porch, about the time when he was young—to use his own words, it was the time in his life when he was "mostly muscle and the rest fool."

"B'ars go to bed about Christmas," he said, "and get up about the middle of April. They make a bed of ivy and twigs in a rock cave. They don't eat endurin' that time, just lay thar suckin' their front paw, so that when they're killed in the spring their guts is just as clean as the inside of yore hand.

"One time a feller I was huntin' with offered to give me the whole hide and half the meat, both, if I'd crawl in a cave whar we figgered a b'ar was and smoke him out. B'ar meat's good. Hit tastes just like beef, and hit sweetened. So I said I'd do it.

"I raked some leaves and twigs together and started a fire just inside the cave. And the b'ar was in thar all right. Only hit didn't seem like thar was room enough for us both, hardly, so the b'ar got out. On hits way hit cuffed the gun out of my hands and knocked me flat, and then clumb out over me. I still got the claw marks. The other feller shot him and give me what he said he would. I was risky in them days."

The deer and the elk that used to be killed in the mountains by the "100" are not nearly so common now, although almost any roadside restaurant or mountain hotel has a pair of glassy-eyed heads mounted on the wall. That they once abounded, however, shows in the frequent place names referring to them, such as Elk Horn City, Banner Elk, Bull Scrape, Buck Creek. Deer Lick is so named because the deer used to come there for salt. Head and Shoulders Mountain is named after a deer that was head and shoulders bigger than any deer ever seen before. It was so big that when it fell, all the streams for miles around grew oily.

There is plentiful lesser game still, including birds. The first tang of fall in the air, the first woodbine to turn scarlet, is the signal for many a man to get out his high-lace boots, call his setter, check his tobacco supply, and take to the hills with his gun—his pulse quickening in anticipation of the whir of grouse wings.

Or it may be the pheasant, scurrying ahead of the hunter's spaniel and then leaving the ground to go hurtling through the branches, that has summoned him to the hill woods.

If it is the soft winnowing of woodcock wings that has called, then no other game bird holds interest. Shakespeare gave the name of that odd drab little bird to the foolish, but it is a quarry that holds a peculiar attraction for the hunter. It is said that once a hunter hears the musical whistle of the woodcock's wings; once that strange little brown creature has scuttled between him and the sun; once on a cold day when the hills are gun metal, the snow being that dark on the northern slopes and he comes upon the whiter chalk marks of the woodcock—he is lost.

The first classical mention of bird shooting, to my knowledge, is in Exodus. The Hebrew children, destined as the chosen people, no sooner were miraculously delivered from Pharoah's bondage than they complained in the wilderness about missing the fleshpots of Egypt. They were not talking about sin. They literally were hungry for the evening pots of bubbling meat stew that they had enjoyed to the full in the land of Egypt. The amazingly patient Lord heard their mumurings against Moses and said to them: "At eventide ye shall eat meat. . . . And it came to pass that at eventide the quails came up and covered the camp."

Today's quail are in far graver danger from the skulking fox than from the occasional hunter who drives eager hundreds of miles to rise in the chill dawn and tramp over unaccustomed stubbly highland fields until chiller dusk. He may glory in the cold burn of tingling health, appreciatively watch the systematic working of the dogs sniffing their zigzag way to stand elegant point at a covey of flushed quail. When the lure of the hills includes the quail's kindred, the ruffed grouse—that plump brown bird skimming safely around the bend of the next hill, or lurking close to the concealing brown earth in rhododendron thickets— the call of the wild pales. Tired as a reedy weed, claiming he aches for six feet although he may be only five feet eleven, the occasional sportsman can hardly wait to get back to that nice warm office.

But the wild turkey—there is nothing like it in all Appalachia. John James Audubon, accredited the finest nature artist in history, who began his career by drawing birds when he was a penniless young man in backwoods Kentucky, gives unstinted praise to "the handsome fowl." In his narrative text in his two-volume *Birds of America* he wrote: "The great size and beauty of the wild turkey, its value as a delicate and highly prized article of food, and the circumstances of its being the origin of the domesticated race on both continents, render it one of the most interesting birds indigenous to the United States."

Audubon assigned the wild turkey the place of honor in his book—the first color illustration of more than four hundred done by the artist's passionately disciplined brush. The painting shows the male, "the great American cock," striding through fallen leaves toned to the same rich bronzes as the cock's folded wings and sweeping tail. The high blue head is arrogantly turned for a look back.

And well it might arrogantly be. Even the most experienced of practical hunters who goes out for wild turkey—you get more meat per bullet, and better—grant that the wary bird is challenging game. The seasonal hunter feels lucky if he so much as sees a wild turkey, usually as it is taking a running start for ponderous flight, its majestic wings spread back against the blazing winter sky.

Down around the Smoke Hole district in West Virginia, a man recently had the misfortune to go to sleep while he was boiling his sorghum into molasses. The huge pot of it represented his whole crop and, when it caught on fire, it made quite a blaze. The neighbors were exceedingly anxious—but not about his sorghum burning up. "I hope Dave didn't skeer all the turkeys out of the country with that fire."

Rattlesnake hunting, in some sections, has a charm. A veteran of Snake Den, named Oaty, told me what to do if I ever came upon a rattlesnake. Of course, Oaty was a liar. It was said of him that he would rather climb a tree and tell a lie than stand on the ground and tell the truth. However, his wife stood up for him indulgently.

"He only lies enough to enjoy hisself," she told me that October afternoon.

We had gone hoping to find a Faith-and-Fortune quilt I was seeking, having heard that Mrs. Oaty had one of rare old pattern. We followed a lane with some chinquapin trees along it. The sweet little brown nuts are a lot of trouble but they are good. The house, when we got to it, was up the hill a ways, beside an oak tree. There is nothing like a mountain oak in October. Its leaves were sparse enough for each leaf, in that first moment we looked up, to be one thing against the clear blue sky before the wind hit.

The house itself was the kind that is held up in front by a couple of bean poles and then leans back against the mountain, so that you cross the porch at a decided pitch. But it was a "very" kind of day—very bright, very windy, very carefree, and although I did not find a Faith-and-Fortune quilt, I found out what to do in case I ever came upon a rattlesnake "quirled" up in the road. Oaty told me. First of all, you want to take yourself some tobacco.

"Just take yoreself a good chaw of fresh, homemade tobacco," recommended Oaty. What made him think of it was a neat brown arc he had just sent out into the October sunshine. He paused to watch the fluid accuracy of its fall and then went on enthusiastically. "And whilst yo're a-workin' out on hit, step over in the bresh and git yoreself a good stout forked stick. Then step back in the road and ram the fork down over the snake's neck— and stomp on hits tail right quick, so hits tail won't smack! Then ease down, and ease down, until you git right close to the snake's mouth—and hit'll be open—and let fly that wad of fresh, homemade tobacco and old mister snake'll roll over on hits back and roll back on hits belly and die dead."

A good many hunting stories that you hear are inclined, like Oaty's, to handle the truth a little carelessly. Percy Mackaye celebrates a Kentucky Baron Munchausen in his *Tall Tales of the Kentucky Hills*. West Virginia has such a one, too, renowned for his yarns that he builds as he goes and that his captivated hearers add to as they pass on. Thus the story of the time Grandpappy Sparks went coon hunting has taken on proportions.

"Now, Grandpappy Sparks," so the story goes, "was jest about the dearest lover of coon huntin' in the world. Thar wasn't nothin' he liked better than to roam the hills with his dogs and his guns, unless hit was to set around and yarn about hit afterward.

"But Grandpappy hadn't been out coon huntin' for oh, two, three years. He'd jest buttocked down in his wheel chair—jest set by hisself by the fire, dour as an old rain crow. He'd been settin' like that ever since the night the ha'nt got in.

"That was the night Grandpappy woke up along about midnight feelin' quare. By the light of the moon shinin' down through a peephole in the roof he seed, down at the foot of his bed, somethin' white and quare, goin' back and forth, back and forth. Grandpappy riz up and drew his gun to him and says: 'Speak, if yo're human.'

"Nothin' heerd.

"Agin Grandpappy says: 'Speak, if yo're human.'

"Nothin' come.

"So Grandpappy tuk aim and fired. Shot off all five of his toes.

"Wal, this kindly crippled him some and jest tuk the heart plumb out of him. So he'd been glummin' thar by the fire, woeful worn and weary like.

"But t'other night he seed his grandsons Hounddog and Squinteye gittin' ready to go coon huntin'. He wheeled hisself over to the door and set thar watchin' 'em a spell, and he couldn't stand hit.

" 'Boys,' he says, 'take me with you! I hain't long for to live and I want to hear them hounds a-givin' tongue jest once agin afore I die.'

" 'Oh, la, no, Grandpappy,' says Hounddog. 'We're goin' way up yonder on top of Hickory Mountain.'

"And Squinteye says, 'Leastwise, Grandpappy, I don't reckon you'd enjoy yoreself much. The last time me and Hounddog went we only got us one coon, and hit was so pore we sot hit on a limb and let hit went.'

"But Grandpappy, he begged and pleaded so powerful pitiful

that finally Hounddog looked at Squinteye and Squinteye looked
at Hounddog and they said: 'Wal' might as wal.'

"So Hounddog, he hitched the dogs to his belt, and Squinteye,
he hitched the lantern and the gun to his'n, and betwixt 'em they
made a kind of cheer and h'isted the old man up into hit. But, la,
long before them boys had got to the top of Hickory Mountain
they war puffin' and pantin' and thar tongues war hangin' out.

"But Grandpappy, he war feelin' pearter. He sot thar a-
laughin' and a-talkin' and a-chucklin' to hisself and havin' a good
old time. When hit looked like the boys war layin' out to set him
down he says: 'Oh boys, don't set me down hyar. Listen to them
hounds a-givin' tongue up thar all in one place! Hit's that old
holler oak! They've treed! Take me up thar, boys—hit hain't
more'n a mile and a half around the shoulder of the mountain.'

"Wal, the boys war too weary to protest. They struggled on—
bammin' into rocks and batterin' through laurel hells, till by the
time they got up to that old holler oak they jest had strength
enough to set Grandpappy down on a log and then fall down
theirselves on their faces.

"But Grandpappy, he set thar a-peekin' and a-peerin', and directly he says: 'Squinteye, shine that old bull's-eye lantern up
thar on that first branch, son. 'Pears to me like thar's two big old
eyes a-shinin' down.'

"Squinteye got up strength enough to rise a little and shine the
lantern—and shore enough, thar war two big old eyes a-shinin'
down!

"Grandpappy war plumb delighted. 'Shine her up thar on that
second branch, son. 'Pears to me like thar's two more big old eyes
a-shinin' down!'

"Squinteye shined the lantern on the second branch and shore
enough—thar war two more big old eyes a-shinin' down.
Grandpappy war plumb excited.

" 'Hounddog, take that gun stick, boy, and rub a sulphur
match on yore hindsights and yore foresights and see can you git
that top feller, and maybe hit'll knock down the bottom one, and

we'll have us two old streaked and striped raccoons with one shot!'

"Wal, Hounddog fired her a crack, keerless like, and la, thar come down out of that tree jest about four-hundred pounds of the maddest West Virginia b'ar you ever seen.

"Thar war considerable confusion.

"Somebody kicked the lantern halfway down the mountain, so they didn't have no light to see by. Hounddog had the gun, but the fightin' war so close he couldn't shoot to do no good. So he tuk the gun in both hands and used hit like a battlin' stick, only he hit Squinteye right acrost the back of the neck with hit and purt nigh knocked his head off.

"Hit warn't three minutes—oh la, hit warn't but two minutes and a half—till them boys could hear the dogs war a-gettin' the worst of hit.

"Hounddog kicked one of the b'ars to turn hits tusks loose from his dog's skull, and with that the rumpus turned into a clawin' match betwixt 'em. The b'ar riz up and give Hounddog a cuff that sent him britch sprawlin'. The dogs tuk to kiyi-in' and yippin' and stickin' their tails betwixt their legs and lightin' out for home. Hounddog jumped up and lit runnin' hisself.

" 'Run, Squinteye, run. And if you can't run, git out of the way of a man what can!'

" 'We can't go without the gun, Hounddog—'

" 'Yonder hit lays,' yelled back Hounddog, 'and you about to tromple hit—'

"Squinteye got the gun and skun down after Hounddog, and neither of 'em never stopped till they got to their own gate. Then they stopped whar they war. Hounddog looked at Squinteye, and Squinteye looked at Hounddog.

" 'Hounddog,' says Squinteye, 'do you know what we've done? We've done left Grandpappy to be et by the b'ars.'

"Hounddog never said a word. He just spit regular for a while. Then he says 'Squinteye, I hate mighty bad to see what we're goin' to see. But the only thing for us to do is to go to the house and git us a basket and go up after the remains.'

"So they went on to the house, their heads a-hangin' down, to git 'em a basket and go back for Grandpappy. The dogs war a-layin' in front of the fire, a-cryin' and lickin' their wounds, the way hounddogs do. And over in his chair set Grandpappy!

" 'Great balls of fire, Grandpappy, how'd you get down hyere?'

" 'Boys,' said Grandpappy, 'I come in ahead of the dogs.' "

Herbs and Bitters

Alek Wiseman age 80 dide marc 20
1877 war farmer & stilde and never had
Dronk boy never had Doc in hos for sick
he ras 12 in family war good hand to
mak brandy

SPRINGTIME in the mountains used to mean a good big dose of cherry-bark bitters and whiskey for everybody in the family, from the granny-woman on down to the least one. It was tasty, toned you up, and was good for the system in general. Yellowroot was another tonic guaranteed to pick anybody up who "wasn't much." Yellowroot, however, was bitter—"Hit was good and bitter."

All the old-time southern mountain women have a traditional knowledge of herb doctoring. No doubt originally it was a knowledge of necessity, since the trained skill of doctors and nurses, and news of the new ways of doing, have come to them only in comparatively recent years.

They listen with interest to minute dramas over the air that urge them to hurry down to the nearest drugstore and buy a box of kidney pills—remembering the times they have hurried to the nearest she-balsam, cut off a hunk of bark, and brewed it into a kidney tea. Some people preferred ivy tea. Sage was the thing for common colds in those days. If the cold went beyond the simple reach of sage and developed into "the pneumonia fever," then pennyroyal was called into use. Pennyroyal also was recommended to anyone bad off with neuralgia.

Many a mountain woman has lain in a darkened room with a nervous headache, treating it with cold packs—of catnip and dock leaves. A poultice of dock leaves could draw the soreness out of boils.

André Michaux made his famous tour of the southern mountains in 1802, incidentally introducing the idea that the ginseng so common to the hillside fields was a highly marketable drug. Until then the mountain women had been digging ginseng in leaf-tinted autumn only for domestic use. While the yellow, aromatic root did not cure what is now called arthritis—"Rheumatiz will hurt you till you die and leave it"—a chaw of " 'sang" somehow warmed and cheered at the same time. Along with ginseng, the mountain women began gathering other roots and herbs whose medicinal qualities had been fireside conversation for generations, trading their yield for goods brought in by pack peddlers, who in turn sold it to outside drug markets.

The Kentucky women claim that the Indians first gave them their knowledge of the medicinal value the woods around them held. It was the mountain men, however, who decided that "Yarbs hain't nary bit of good without jest the least grain of whiskey."

Sometimes it took more than a least grain. Huge doses of apple brandy were administered after an emetic taken in cases of "milk silk," a dreaded illness caused from milk poisoned by cows grazing in too shady places.

Puffballs, it was held by some, were the proper thing to bind on an open wound. If the mushroom-like plants that burst into brown powder at a touch were out of season, cobweb was substituted, or even soot. The more expert, especially hunters or woodcutters accustomed to dealing with emergencies far from the home base, scotched this whole school of thought. "You don't want to go devilin' around in a wound at all! Blood's the best dressin' a wound can have."

The garden also was made to yield itself to the sickroom. Fried onions with goat "taller" poured over them made a salve that could be rubbed on the throat of a child with croup. Flaxseed and honey were used for whooping cough. A little poke of

3

Moonshining was a "mort of trouble, and risky."

At the mill, you could get corn ground on shares.

4   Jacob Carpenter, scribe of Blue Ridge life and death.

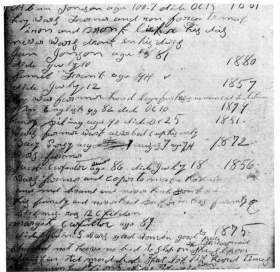

5

(Left and opposite)
On ledger pages,
the name, the date,
the deceased's
way of life.

Sometimes the hand-carved stone said simply, "Gone but . . ."

6   *"Kneel ye down, oh kneel ye down,*
And choose the prettiest girl in town."

asafetida tied around a child's neck kept away disease in general —working on the principle, no doubt, that the smell of it would keep anyone with a disease at a distance—as well as check the approach of everybody else.

Asafetida and whiskey brewed into a tea was downed as a hopeful relief for itching hives. If that didn't work, you *could* use the white powdery substance off the top of hen manure.

Shingles were cured by bathing the irritated portions of the skin with the fresh warm blood of a black chicken. For diphtheria, a common toad was sometimes split open and bound to the throat—quickly, again while the blood was still warm.

There is an element of sense in these homemade remedies. A few, however, were sheer superstition. If someone was to be taken with fits, for instance, just bore a hole in a tree, shave the hair from the armpits of the afflicted person, put the hair in the hole, then plug it up.

The superstitious cures for warts are many and well known, being spread over wider areas than the mountain confines: Gather as many pebbles as you have warts, make a bundle of them, and drop them in the road—whoever picks up the bundle will get your warts; Steal somebody's dishrag and rub it over your warts; Plant as many beans in a circle as you number warts —when the beans grow, your warts will go.

Hemorrhage was taken care of by driving a double-bitted ax into the floor under the bed of the person who was bleeding. Thus many a woman in childbirth has died.

And many a woman in childbirth has died because ignorance and the lack of care accompanying even the sounder home remedies have had to substitute for skilled medical aid. Each midwife, of course, had her own authoritative variations of the nothing she could do. Some claimed that if the woman lay on her side and "hollered," it helped the child to come. Others used very strong doses of hot pepper tea to "fetch on this child-thing." Still others made the mother sit bolt upright during the whole of labor. Uremic infection was avoided (it was hoped) by having the mother lie for three hours in the afterbirth before the bedding was changed. In the meantime, the baby just "cotched" was held upside down and shaken by its heels so its liver wouldn't grow to its sides. After the abrupt introduction into the topsy-turvy world in which it had miraculously managed to arrive, it was righted dazedly and soothed by a little catnip tea. If the digestive system seemed for some reason a little awry after all that and it developed a rash (called the "thrash": two varieties—red and brown), that was taken care of by calling in a man who had never seen his own father to come blow his breath down the tender young throat.

But whatever the hazards of "childing"—as Shakespeare and the mountain people put it—the new baby itself is the most welcomed thing on earth.

"A baby's always somethin' new in the house," one young mother told me gently. "The children love so good to play with hit." She was still lying weakly in bed. She had almost died during this last childbirth—a matter she dismissed as of no importance now.

"That kind of pain is easiest forgot in the world." At that moment she was looking on happily as her husband bent to take up the child from the cradling crook of her arm, with the warm sweet feel of it in his own arms betraying itself on his lean face.

Mountain men as a class are devoted family men. They would do anything for their "babies"—it has been merely a question of knowing the right thing to do.

Too often, the few native doctors in earlier times were as uninformed about their practice as were their patients, according to the stories of their "cures" that survive them. Occasionally, however, you find the hill version of the old-fashioned country doctor with a little professional education and a great deal of good sense. One of these told me there were two things important to being a doctor: the first was to diagnose; the second was to use horse sense.

He still is practicing, and people of three West Virginia counties depend upon him in faith—with their faith founded on fifty years of his whittling out this one's appendix and rolling up his pants to wade the creek when the ice was floating to go bring on that one's baby. His records show he has brought over a thousand babies into the world, only eight of those times with the help of a registered nurse. He depended on whatever help was at hand, I gathered from one of his graphic accounts. It concerned a stubborn maternity case in which, as a last resort, he was preparing to take the child. He commandeered the services of a neighbor, an Aunt Deedy who tipped the scale at around two hundred. The big old woman was bending over the bed to give the anaesthetic for him, holding the chloroform rag under the patient's nose, when "b' God," swore the doctor, at the crucial moment "over Deedy went!"

"I looked up and thar Deedy lay, stretched out cold on the floor. Nobody else was thar except the husband, and he was wanderin' in and out of the house, lettin' in drafts, half out of his head with worry. But just then I heard the mailman drive up. I stuck my head out the door and hollered, 'Homer, yo're just the feller I need. Nobody in here's worth a damn.' I got the chloroform rag and knocked the patient out myself this time, and when Homer come in I said, 'Grab aholt of that leg thar.'

" 'Oh my soul alive,' gasped Homer. 'I never seen the like!'

" 'You ain't supposed to see! You're just supposed to keep aholt!' "

The baby arrived safely and the mother did nicely.

Mountain people are usually as heroic in bearing their own pain as they are seemingly indifferent to that of other people. Such stoicism is a part of the fatalism that seemed to find a natural home in the mountains. It has let highlanders sit helplessly by the bedside, accepting death before it came: "What is to be, will be."

It let an old uncle, who lived over the hill from the school where I was teaching, come in the store at mail time one morning, get his Sears and Roebuck catalogue, and stand around letting a good little bit of the day go by before he gave out the news of his wife's illness. Then he mentioned, "Poppy's ailin'."

The next morning he reported, "Poppy's gittin' worse."

The third morning he said it wouldn't surprise him much if she was "tuk." The next morning, as he had expected, she was dead. He shook his head about it. He said he didn't seem to have real good luck with his women, although he had begun at a right young age. This was his third.

In spite of this attitude of fatalism, in spite of the dependency on home remedies, despite the often tragic results of ignorance and superstition, the southern mountain people have persisted in remaining a sturdy lot.

"We didn't use to know nothin' up hyere in the mountains," an old North Carolina man admitted to me cheerfully, "except that we were a-livin'."

That they lived at all, and to the ripe old age that many of them did, is astonishing by today's hygienic standards. But there was nothing novel, nothing strange about longevity in the Spartan highlands. True, before a Revolutionary War veteran lost his battle with the Angel of Death at the age of 113, the neighbors did begin to say good-humoredly, "We're goin' to have to shoot that old soldier again to kill him."

And only a few years ago a West Virginian told us with amusement about going to the funeral of an aunt in the little town of Hundred, named for his great-great-grandfather who lived to be 107. His grandparents were in their nineties. As they stood sadly together beside the casket, Ollie heard his grandmother say to his grandfather, "I knowed we'd never raise her. She always was sickly." The dear departed was 67.

Except for the mountain sections that particularly suffered from invasion during the Civil War, when sometimes all they had left was "one milk cow we hid in the cellar," there never has been any necessity for anyone with a garden patch in the back yard to go hungry—even though "garden sass" was no great favorite with the menfolk. While they preferred the meat they hunted down themselves, hogs turned loose to fend for themselves in the woods were no trouble and bred like rabbits. Meat of any variety is still apt to be fried to a state that caused an outlander fisherman, who didn't feel so well after a hearty breakfast of mountain-fried ham and eggs, to confide to a rod-and-reel companion, "I've often wondered what happened to all the old tennis shoes. Now I know."

In turn, sinewy highlanders are privately amazed and amused at outlanders who eat "worlds and worlds more than a body needs." Their natural hardihood can also be largely attributed to their love for pure air and pure water amounting to an obsession. The door is not left standing open because somebody forgot to shut it but because the people indoors want breath to breathe. And they take a connoisseur's pride in their water and are demanding about its quality. A spring must come up in that silent clarity that only springs do whose source lies deep. If it is branch water they drink, it must come from some stream running through laurel and rock, or filtered by the hemlocks dipping in their shadows, so that the water comes sparkling to the sun, achingly cold in its purity.

Pure air and pure water and the cures of nature—the heart stimulant digitalis from the purple foxglove, creosote from the wood tar of the pine or the beech for bronchitis and coughs, belladonna from the deadly nightshade plant for pain of inflammation and constipation, arnica from the dried flowers of the Leopard's-bane for bruises and cuts, pokeroot for eczema, oil of thyme for diphtheria and typhoid, hemlock to relieve the pain of cancer, jimson root for ulcers and to help palsy, wolfbane root for fevers, sassafras and bonesake and snakeroot for tonics, prickly ash and the white oak and the blackberry root for tannic acid, clover for salves and astringents, bloodroot for corns—they have gone to the woods for them. We buy them over the counter.

Women's Little Ways

Liz Franklin age 72 dide aug 29 1889
ware niz lady to anibodi she like

"THAR'S only two places for a woman," said a mountain man of the old school comfortably. "One's in the kitchen and t'other's in the featherbed."

And it is true that from time beyond question it has been a deep-seated matter of fact that the southern highland man is lord and master. A woman's finer sensibilities, if they happen to come within his notice at all, are more apt to annoy him than anything else. He is impatient with a woman he has to "gentle and hand feed."

Once I was watching one of these sturdy old lords, who had outlived four women, splicing a piece of deerhide into shoestrings. As he made the unhurried, expert splices he told me about the household of his youth. There were twelve boys in the family, and in the course of the years his father adopted fourteen more. His mother and his two sisters constituted the female contingent.

"My gracious!" I exclaimed. "Wasn't that a lot of work for just three women, taking care of all those men?"

"Why la no," he answered in honest surprise. "Hit warn't no work, much. Oh, they aimed to weave us a pair of pants apiece a year, and a couple of shirts. And if they got bad tore, they sewed 'em up ag'in. But they didn't have no bother with their own clothes. They warn't goin' noplace. And they didn't have to fuss about the house. They didn't have no curtains.

"The cookin' was easy. Oh, they'd keep a mess of corn bread baked up for anybody who felt the urge. And come summer, now and ag'in they'd cook up a mess of garden sass. But we didn't keer for that much. Mostly we'd just go out to the smokehouse and cut us off a hunk of meat and et as we walked.

"And they didn't have no washin'," he finished simply, "because we didn't wear no socks."

He forgot about their outdoor chores. All mountain women enjoy working in the flower beds and gardens. But in the time when gathering fodder, helping plow, and splitting kindling were added to her natural pleasure in planting things and watching them grow, her early aging days got "a least might wearisome."

It seldom occurs to the mountain man to say or do the little things that please a woman. And occasionally she gets beaten. Even though the men are fond of their families, they have considered this a traditional part of their duty as head of the house. One woman told me earnestly of a particularly stern father and husband: "He was a good man. If me or the children ever took a crooked step, he'd whip us." When she looked at her man, her eyes had respect. In fact, a mountain woman would have little regard for a man who did not lord it over her.

Yet despite their submission, mountain women, like women the world over, have their little ways.

Sometimes it takes to eternity and the next generation to see their wishes fulfilled, as in the case of the worn-down woman who departed her life as meekly as she had endured it, reduced to making no protest about anything. Her husband did not bother to commemorate the departure with a funeral service. Then he, the lowly one's husband, died. Always a demanding sort, for him the best of graveyard meetings was promptly planned. The thirteen-year-old boy of the house was hustled to ask the preacher to come "improve the funeral occasion." His mother had died the year before, just when there was something about the hurt look at the back of her shy blue eyes that was beginning to make him love her fiercely. He had stood in the room stupidly and watched her go, completely frightened, and afterward had used all his strength to keep from sobbing there among the others who did not know what grief was.

"We'd take it kindly," he recited to the preacher when he was sent about his father, "if you'd give the oration." He'd been warned to be mannerly. The preacher said he was proud to be asked. The deceased had been a prominent man.

"And while yo're a-funeralin' Pa," said the boy, come early into that nonchalance that masks iron, "say a few words about Ma too, will you? And say Ma's first."

There are, of course, exceptions. When I first knew Uncle Nick, he and Aunt Charity were growing old together and they seemed to find it not a bad experience at all. They had the quiet about them that lets two people who have found satisfaction in each other view the rest of the world with tolerance. They had had their ups and downs in their time, according to their accounts. When it had been a crest, they had ridden it, but when it had not been, they had roughed it. Either way, they evidently had had a pretty good time together. Aunt Charity always had thought, and still did, that the best thing she had ever done was marry Nick. And Nick still considered Charity a privilege and a pleasure.

Many a time, the neighbors growing up around the old couple would smile a little, in that way you do at a small thing that is thoroughly nice. They would smile to see Uncle Nick climbing slowly up a slope toward the flame of a wild azalea. A "flower pot," he called it, for Charity. Charity loved flowers.

But there still is the North Carolina woman who got "so plumb wore out with the no-account ways of her fam-il-ee, that she just tuk to the bed and stayed thar, year in and year out, just gittin' up ever' now and then to give 'em all a good thrashin'!"

The Devil's Wife

Franky Carpenter age 56 dide oc 25
1862 hard workin womin on farm made
corn oates

THE high winding road had rounded a curve in the clear dark of great trees and then, there ahead, lay the town, in moonlight and mist on a Saturday night, and it was mine.

As an excuse to stay, I taught in the school. Since then the school has greatly improved and is more particular about pedagogic qualifications. But it was a high-hearted experience for everyone concerned, and early in it I became aware that the people living in our southern hills have a unique contribution to make to our national literature, in the form of a mythology. It takes time and loneliness to make mythology, and nights when even so sure a thing as a mountain wall is no more than a mark in a dream. It takes hunger. And historic imagination.

Our highlanders happened to have been well stocked with the ingredients for a mythology. Rooted in the long-gone past, raised up in the raw ways of a young country, they have struck out something new—different from anything in America, yet peculiarly American.

My first experience with it came one morning when I found myself confronted with such mathematical paralyzers as, "If an ice factory makes ice in half-ton cakes, how fast does the ice melt in thirty minutes?"—or problems equally unfathomable. I was writing a wild undercover note to the seventh-grade teacher for help again, when Ingaby came up to the desk.

Ingaby had bright blue eyes and fair hair, skinned back tight
from an alert little face. She had a quick mind and usually a
merry one. But this morning she was solemn, with her solemnity
carrying an extra load of importance.

"My Aunt May died."

Not knowing her Aunt May, still I looked up, of course, and
made the perfunctory expression of sympathy. "Oh, that's too
bad. What was the matter?"

"She got spelled and turned fitified," said the child simply. I
looked at her blankly. She nodded.

"The old witch on yon side of the mountain done hit."

"Did it," I corrected automatically, hitting on the one thing I
could be sure of at the moment.

"Did it," said Ingaby dutifully. Then she added, "She's the
very one all right!" She grew sad. "And Aunt May used to be the
prettiest woman to look at in the face!"

"Really?" By this time I was even more mystified by Aunt
May than by the ice factory, and much more interested.

So Ingaby told me, her bright eyes on fire, a little girl in a
very clean calico dress repeating some tale from home. As she
told it, her childish voice took on a lilting sweetness, minored
with plaintiveness. That strangely fascinating quality of voice
also was something she had come into from hearing a long time
back.

"The old witch was jealous. She wanted Aunt May's man for
her own daughter. And one night when Aunt May's man was out
coon huntin', the old witch come over and into the house. And
she made Aunt May eat nine witch balls, made out of nine
needles all wrapped around with fine little hair. Then she turned
Aunt May into a horse and rid her up and down the Valley.
Every night and every night, my mother said, she done hit . . .
did it . . . till the once beautiful woman got poorly, and ugly,
and turned fitified."

"Well . . ." I said inadequately. It was the first witch story I
had ever heard; a few days after, I went home with Ingaby to
call.

If she had not shown me, I could not have found my way there alone. We went up the hill from the schoolhouse and dropped down the other side to a hollow that fingered out deviously. She knew which way to choose and we followed that creek clear to its head. Sometimes we were in the creek bed, but more often on a narrow path beside it. It was the kind of path where rhododendron and scrub oak and blackberries close in quickly, letting you see only a little at a time ahead or behind you; even the creek beside you is known only by its sound on the rocks, like feelings too clear to be thought, and shortly all sense of familiar things is left behind you and lost, so that you marvel again—even on a narrow path with no vista—"Wild, wild country still!" The witch story did not seem so incongruous here.

Ingaby had said her Aunt May once had been a beautiful woman. So had her mother, hauntingly so. Plenty of meat and potatoes, for Ingaby's was a good farm, but still her mother was hungry. She kept looking at me—not at me, but at the unknown life that lay beyond the narrow work-worn boundaries of her own. Dreams that had gone empty looked with tired blue eyes from under the brim of the man's hat she wore. I turned from her to the man, wondering what he was thinking about as he sat with his chair tilted back against the house wall staring at the opposite bank of the creek, and decided not much.

I had brought a present for the "least one," a little boy about four. He and Ingaby were the last children left at home, and Ingaby, with the older one's invariable pleasure in the younger, had told me about him. It was not a particularly appropriate present but the best my belongings offered, a paper weight in the form of a wild young glass horse.

The little boy, who had drawn back shyly close to his mother's drab skirts, took the package silently, not knowing what to do with it.

"Look what for a present the teacher fotched you," encouraged his mother, pleased herself.

He opened the first layers of white tissue strangely and did not seem surprised when nothing showed up. I had to urge him to keep on unwrapping. When the little glass horse finally revealed itself, he looked at it and handed it back. When I assured him it was his, he ran a grubby finger over it awkwardly, giving the promise of knowing it more intimately with time—like a small bud that would open slowly and with a wonder it would never lose. Then all at once he let loose. He flew around gathering up chairs from all over the house, although each of us already had one. He came out carrying one on his head. He was like a quick, tickled little animal.

His mother watched the antics that showed his delight, smiling a little but with a heavy kind of wistfulness attending the smile. She sat holding the little crystalline horse for him carefully and quite as though it were his and none of hers—as though for her it was too late. Once, as we sat on the long porch talking, when Ingaby was telling something about the school that held the excitement of wide horizons, the woman lifted her hand and restlessly pushed back her hair; then she seemed to grow tired all the way through, exhausted by a hint of great things she would never know.

The world of fact and science and philosophy and art was unfolding to Ingaby, as the tissue wrappings had opened up before the younger child. But for their mother, up in that wild shut-in, there was no such promise. She was a "hard-working woman on the farm," and the only way she knew to break the monotony of that, the hard sameness it had fallen into, was the way her people before her had done—imbuing with drama from the days of the Witch of Endor such present squalid circumstances as a woman dying with fits.

The people of our southern mountains have stepped aside to let two centuries go by. But sitting on the porch of the old house, which itself had been there "right at a hundred years," I had a strange sense of time kaleidoscoping; the mother standing back still, but watching her children stepping out into line again, to take their place in the procession of the world.

They enter it with much to contribute from their long seclusion, and if the old lore is one of the minor contributions, it is a flavorsome one.

What other part of the country except the thin air of the mountains—sometimes smelling so sharply of nothing, sometimes "stinking so spicy"—could have nourished such an extravaganza as Skilly Pendergast originated in the outhouse? Her man was away to the widow Lance's, looking at the widow's brindle cow again, and Skilly was starting to cook supper when she heard the fiddle music in the outhouse and lots of people dancing.

She didn't have much wood in the house but she put it all on the fire to have light, and who should she see coming in but the Devil, and four little devils and nine of the prettiest-dressed women she had ever seen, and a whole pack of hellcats. The Devil's wife put apple dumplings on the table.

"Lord, I didn't know where they'd got those dumplings," Skilly would say afterward. "They were big as my fist!" The Devil asked her to eat with them, but she wouldn't.

After the Devil had finished eating and was feeling good, he laid the fiddle across his knee and sawed on it. The Devil's wife opened up the waists of the nine pretty women and made a cross on each of their breasts. Then they all danced. The little devils were playing around the hearthrocks, so close to the fire that Skilly said, "You little devils, you'll git burnt up!"

They didn't answer her. Skilly liked to have an answer when she spoke to people. It made her mad when they didn't pay any attention to her. So she took off her shoe and flung it at them. They all turned on her and made the awfulest faces ever she saw.

"Some people," she reported afterward, "say thar hain't no children in Hell. But thar shore war four little devils in my house that night!"

Then the hellcats began snooping around till she didn't feel to stand for that either. So she threw a kettleful of boiling water at them. But they arched their backs and the water rolled off steam. The house got so steamed up she couldn't see her hand before her face, and the air so flavored with brimstone she couldn't fetch breath.

When it cleared, the Devil and the Devil's wife and the little devils and the nine pretty-dressed women had all disappeared.

But Skilly knew she had got a vision of some sort. She studied on it, and when her man came on in home, she told him about it. He was just about the uneasiest man she had ever seen.

"Skilly, you just drempt hit," he sputtered.

"How could I a-drempt hit," she retorted, "when I used up ary stick of light wood to see 'em by?" Then she said, careless like, "Well, did you git the widow's cow bought?"

"No, I didn't," fumbled Harry. "Because hit was a-comin' on toward dark by the time I got over thar. I figgered, maybe, I'd just step over and give her another look tomorrow."

"Who?" asked Skilly sweetly. "The widow's brindle or the widow?" Then she lit into him. "I can fair see you out in that pasture, a-lookin' at the widow's brindle and then a-lookin' at the widow."

"Now, Skilly," protested Harry. But she cut him short.

"I'm a-leavin', that's what," she told him. "Hit's been give to me in a vision that I've been livin' with a man a-goin' on in sin."

"Skilly, hold on—"

But Skilly wouldn't hold on. She went to a neighbor's house and told her tale. "The devils have routed me," she told them.

The need for something new to talk about acted like tinder and sympathy for Skilly like spark, and they burned together. And Skilly, quick anyhow, took advantage of the flare to strike a pose. She began to claim to see things other people could not. She did seem to have a knack for bringing out the half-thoughts in the lurking places of everybody's mind, and it was a talent that grew with her use of it. She lived with first one neighbor and then another, and they were glad to have her. Long evenings picked up when Skilly Pendergast was there to tell her tales.

In course of time, Harry tried to get Skilly to come back to him. He had married the widow but she had died. At the funeral, somebody ventured with awe, "I'll 'low Skilly Pendergast put hit into the Lord's head to do that—just out of punishment to Harry." The man to whom this was said was disgusted. He said back sarcastically, "I don't reckon the Lord's takin' orders from Skilly Pendergast. Not yet awhile, nohow." But the other was not convinced. "Um mebbe not. But I wouldn't put hit past her to use her influence."

When Harry asked her to come back, Skilly studied him like she was pondering it. He wasn't a bad-looking man, although he could have shaved up and looked better. But finally she told him she guessed she wouldn't. She was making her own way now and getting along good. When she'd lived with him there was nothing about her more than another. But now she had prestige. It was a prestige she kept clear to the end.

She was staying at Jake Taylor's place at the time, and was out at the side of the house washing clothes. Suddenly Jake's wife heard a queer sound and looked out, and there was Skilly, standing on her head in the washtub!

They got her out and stretched her on the ground and crushed on her ribs. But she hadn't drowned. When the doctor got there he said she'd had a stroke. The Taylors figured she must have felt it coming on and knew she was heading for the tub, and betwitched herself so she wouldn't drown. Because when they took the snuff stick out of her mouth, it was dry!

It is an elemental mythology of the soil that our southern mountains have created for us, sometimes romantic, sometimes brutal, often humorous, always restless—a substitute for the life-want set deep in everybody from the beginning, which those of the world can lull with worldly things but which those out of reach of the world have to go down into themselves to satisfy.

Martha Thomas was one of those women made for a strong man. And from the name her husband left behind him, Arzy Thomas was dangerous enough. But his danger lay in the devastation that can be wrought by a little mind. Any capabilities Martha may have had for being a great woman got sapped out of her in little ways. And something of all that had been wanting in her living with Arzy Thomas she put contemptuously into the telling of his dying. Her voice was deliberate, with that ominous quiet that holds back power.

"I knowed he war a-goin' because all the dogs from fur and

nigh come around and howled. The cows come down out of the
woods to the barn lot and lowed and lowed. I went to the door
and looked out. White chickens war a-scratchin' on the doorstone
and la, we didn't have a white chicken on the place!

"Hit war a dark night. But plain as day, comin' down yon side
the mountain, through bresh so thickety a butcher knife couldn't
cut hit, I seed the Devil a-comin'. He war ridin' a coal-black cart,
drivin' coal-black oxen. The cart come down to the door—and
stopped. When it come"—the voice releasing its power now, the
tones going straight down the scale to cold depths and scraping
on the bitter bottom—"hit come empty. But when hit went away
hit had a big black ball in hit that war Arzy's soul."

Naturally, some of these experiences with the supernatural are
vouched for by people who would let anything else that came
along do for thinking. It was a nervously wrinkled little woman
who introduced me to the idea that if anyone ever tried to borrow
anything, you had to be careful, because the borrower might do
you harm. She told me that one day a neighbor woman came to
the house to borrow a blow of soda, but she made an excuse not
to lend it. The neighbor came back three times and finally just
grabbed up the soda and ran.

"And what happened?" I asked.

She got a dimly harassed look. "That's what I ain't never been
sartin about."

She was not certain about anything, including herself. Even
when she sat down, she would sit not quite in the middle of the
chair seat and then look dimly troubled, as though wondering
why the seat didn't feel right. It was easy to imagine that she'd
been a little off center, always, about everything—a little off
center and wondering why life didn't feel quite sure.

Then there was a lurid account in a rapid undertone in which
the teller went to extraordinary lengths to be ordinary, about a
great big old fleshy girl—"La, her big dinners!"—who got be-
witched and her stomach just swelled and swelled. The particular details of her bewitchment I've forgotten, except for the wild
eyes in the old woman who told it and the snuff that dripped
down from each corner of her loose mouth.

It was, however, in the living room of an attractive modern
bungalow in a rapidly changing mountain community—which
the up-and-coming members of that house were helping to
change—that I learned the proper way to do away with a witch.
You draw the witch's picture on the gatepost and then shoot the
picture through the heart with a silver bullet. The young woman
who told me this is thoroughly intelligent, with a quick sense of
humor and an enviable verve of expression. She told me the old
stories because she knew I was interested—casting off any belief
in them herself and yet somehow their substance being still in
them.

"Sometimes when we were little," she said, "people would sit
around at night and tell those tales. Mother'd never let us listen.
But we'd peek down and hear."

That any of the old lore has survived the sweeping changes the
last quarter of a century has made in the mountains is due to the
mountain people's natural ability at storytelling. They tell the old
stories easily, unself-consciously, and with an instinctive eye for
the dramatic. And they delight in an audience—if the audience is
sympathetic and responsive. On the other hand, one of the best
raconteurs I know, a veritable "tale-tellin' devil charmer,"
stopped short at an exchange of amused glances between two of
his listeners. He shut up like a burr and thereafter did not bother
to put himself out about them.

They were guests at the summer resort where he was "helping," and had asked him to tell the story. He had been quite willing to do so, if it would please them and make their visit more
enjoyable. Mountain people are interested in outsiders and feel a
natural friendliness toward them—until they feel they are being
imposed upon or made sport of. Then they draw back into a reserve. If the outsider mistakes this for backwardness he is making a foolish mistake. The highlander withdraws into a sense of
his own dignity as instinctive as his sense of the dramatic, and
regards the less well-bred outsider now with a complete disinter-
est.

The story the summer people interrupted was an old murder
tale of the district, which the teller had heard from his father. It

concerned a man named Asa Meters, who claimed that one day while he and his brother were out shearing sheep, his brother fell off the sled and the upturned shears went through his heart.

Nobody believed him. People did not "confidence" Asa Meters. Mountain people are used to earnestness of purpose being masked under a leisurely detachment. Asa was a small-eyed driver. And his driving determination to get ahead bothered them. When his brother was killed, everybody thought Asa had done it so he would get his brother's share of the property. They thought this showed in his face. They would look at his hands as though they were full of blood.

But nobody could prove his guilt and the brother was buried up in a field back of the house. There was not even the dark dignity of a cedar planted, to mark the place. In course of time Asa decided to turn the field for rye and make some money out of it. He got Henry Holt to come plow for him.

The dead man had been buried in a shallow grave and when Henry, with his bull-tongued plow, came upon it, he pondered the matter and decided what to do.

A proven way to find a murderer is to place the murdered person's skull above the suspect's head, high up and out of reach of water. Then, when the question is put, there is no power in the suspect to lie out of it. On some pretext, Henry got the skull up into Asa's loft, near the fireplace. Then he watched, and when Asa went under it to fix the fire, he accused him.

Asa neither denied nor affirmed the accusation. But he began to shake. It seemed he would shake himself to death. After that he could never eat because, every time he'd try, the vapor of his brother would grab the food away. He couldn't lie down to sleep because his brother's ghost would throw itself down on top of him and smother him. He could only sit by the fire and try to beat his brother's ghost with a stick. A gray something hovered over him all the time, all the time.

Nobody called the law. Nobody felt there was any need. Nature was administering due justice.

That story came out of a group of people who had brought

into the mountain wilderness with them, along with other strong
colonial traits, dislike of the British courts. Through their taxation experience, they had come to mistrust all authority except
that of natural justice. And often a touch of the supernatural, as
in the case of Asa Meters, helped the course along.

Needless to say, even in the early times there were many
people who would scorn interest in any such supernatural nonsense. Saying that mountain people natively are superstitious is
like saying hemlocks are native to the mountains. They are. Yet
there are many places where there are no hemlocks. Sometimes
you can go for a long way through an oak woods where each tree
stands in its own dignity with no underbrush except rhododendron—the rhododendron, too, growing there singly and immacu-
late. Then there are the chestnut knolls where the bears come to
feed. Or there are fields with white rocks like sheep in them.
There are no hemlocks in these places. Yet hemlocks grow in the
mountains, and so do the superstitions of early America; time
before that, they have rooted and grown up there.

Much of the southern mountain legend can be traced very directly back to the legend of England and Scotland and Ireland.
In comparing mythologies, you will find a legendary dog of
West England called the Spectre Hound. It was a fearful thing
to see, evidently. Sir Walter Scott has it as a paralyzing spec-
tacle. "For he was speechless, ghastly wan: Who spoke the
Spectre Hound of Man."

The English dog was shaggy and black, with long black tail
and ears. The American variety is yellow and spotted, and not so
terrorizing. At least one man who was telling me about it said his
father had seen it many a time when he was riding back from
Morganton after salt, and it was company along the lonesome
road.

He said the yellow dog would appear out of nowhere, and for
a while follow along like any ordinary little old dog. Then,
slowly, it would rise and run along in the air. For a time it would
run along beside him, then gradually would skim forward to a
place beside the horse's head.

The old-time terror of a baby dying if it is not baptized was not only a doctrinal part of the Presbyterianism of many of the mountain peoples' forebears, but also wound back to Irish and German folklore. The old Gaelic belief was that unbaptized infants wandered the air till Judgment Day, wailing in distress. The German idea incorporated a mysterious lady known as Frau Bertha, attended by those troops of unbaptized children who formed "the wild huntsmen of the sky." Sometimes an old crone, on stormy days in the mountains, can hear their wail and peer out to see them sweeping homelessly across the dreary sky on the cold wintry winds.

The fires of a real mountain house are never allowed to go out. The fact that, had they been allowed to go out in the old days, someone in the household would probably have had to walk miles to borrow fire to light them again, is no doubt a very sound functional basis for the habit. However, the highland fires of Scotland and Ireland were not allowed to go out either. The hearth traditionally is a sacred place—a place of warmth and security, the center of the home.

In that regard there is another ghost story about a household that was roused every morning by a scraping sound across the hearthstone. The mother's eyes glistened as she told about it. She said it was the ghost of her man, come back to scrape away the night ashes and freshen the fire for his homefolks. He always had been good to them, and every morning he still came back to fix the fire.

I heard the story about the sawmill ghost one morning while I was waiting for the mail at the store. The general store of any mountain town—and often the store is about all the town there is—is a good place to find a guide for hunting, or to get information about fishing or homespun. But most of all it is a place to sit and rest yourself.

Mountain people never at any time appear to feel pressed by the necessity of making a living, but at mailtime they drift into the store to wait as though they could wait all day and all night and tomorrow morning, and have a very pleasant time doing it. To someone from the strained world outside that is always in a hurry, this leisurely social hour in the middle of the morning may be a matter of amazement, scorn, envy, or habit—depending on how long you can stay.

This particular June morning the sky overhead was fire-blue and the mud out front was cracking open and loving it. Everybody was loafing around in the sunshine as though it were, as one ruddy blond in overalls, leaning in the doorway, expressed it, "just come day, go day, without a thing on earth to study about." A little boy named Jerkwater got a man started on the mill story. The man had handlebar mustaches and a couple of mild black devils for eyes, and was taking his ease on a bench against the store wall.

Jerkwater's freckles were so thick his cheeks were mustard brown, and what brought on the story was that Jerkwater had divulged to his chums out front that he had a penny to spend. They all came trooping up the store steps to help him spend it.

"Git horehound, Jerkwater," one of the little boys was urging in strident whispers, although there was little else he could have gotten, the store being "fresh out" of almost everything—a regretful piece of information that the storekeeper gave out philosophically, without excuse or offer of substitution.

"A stick of horehound," teased one of the men on the store porch, "will last you a week, Jerkwater, and you suck light on hit."

At that, Jerkwater, in an agony of grinning embarrassment, let the penny slip through his fingers. It rolled gaily off the porch and all the little boys scurried to find it.

"You shoulda spent that penny, son, afore hit got away from you."

"Why, certainly he should have."

For a few minutes lazy wit was free and everyone enjoyed himself immensely at the mild expense of Jerkwater. Then the mustaches leaned down over the edge of the porch and got themselves a piece of hay from a clump growing wild there and nibbled at it, and the man behind them said that reminded him of the time Dave Kinder let a fortune get away from him.

It seemed Dave Kinder himself had never seen the ghost at the sawmill that was a couple of miles up the road. Neither had anyone else. But a few people had said they heard it. Riding by, they claimed they could hear it shivering in the night. It was the ghost of a man who had been drowned in the cold millstream. The stream is held back by a dam at the side of the mill, so that the water there lies still and dark, deep and sufficient—until those moonless nights when the invisible ghost rises up out of it to shake terribly.

The mill got itself haunted years ago by a man traveling north on foot. Nobody knew who he was or a thing about him. But he had a little sack of something so heavy he could hardly carry it. There was some talk of its being gold. He spent the night in the mill, and it was bruited around afterward he had been killed there, for nobody ever saw him again. But people going past the mill on dark nights began to hear that blood-churning sound of shivering.

One night Dave Kinder took him a good slug of corn and said he wasn't afeared. He was going to go in that mill, just to see what the hell a ghost was like. He took a lantern with him and some sulphur matches, but he didn't figure on fetching light till he heard something to make it worthwhile. That shivering noise took up. Though he was waiting for it, when it came his hair rose straight up on his head and his chin whiskers like to pulled spang out. Dave said it was the awfulest sound ever he heard! He said he couldn't understand why he'd ever wanted to come in there in the first place—and then, by golly, there came another sound! A kind of little rattling all around his feet! He got that placed, though, directly. That was the sulphur matches dropping one by one from his shaking hands. He made out to get the lantern lit . . . and then liked to died.

The shivering had ceased, but someone was coming. He could hear the slow footsteps, coming nearer and nearer; nearer still. When they stopped, whatever it was was right alongside him. Well, Dave finally got up strength enough to raise his eyes to look; there stood the dripping remains. The eyes were great sunken stares and the flesh was all rotting away. The mouth was open and Dave got a good view of the teeth and the blue purplish gums. The teeth looked about to fall out. Dave said the whole thing just looked like a corpse that had laid in the river and then got up and was walking around.

"In the name of the Father and Son and the Holy Ghost, who are you?" quavered Dave—using the ancient idea of referring to the Deity when talking to a ghost.

The ghost didn't answer flat out but led the way through the mill and up back of it into the brush, and pointed to a spot on the ground. Dave marked the spot with a honeysuckle stick and then got himself out of the place as fast as his tottering legs would take him.

"I'm drunk," he said hopefully to his wife. "I couldn't hold my pint and I've the ague and I'm a-goin' to go lay down." Then he told her all that happened.

"You're not drunk!" His wife was plumb delighted. "You've just found yoreself a fortune! I'll lay to hit that whoever killed that traveler got scared out and buried the money and run. That ghost was tryin' to tell you whar the money is buried at! You go get in the bed and take a good sleep and in the mornin' I'll help you dig."

The next morning they went back to the spot and, sure enough, there the honeysuckle stick was, still stuck in the ground. Dave figured he hadn't been drunk after all and maybe his wife was right for once, and they started in to dig, he and his wife both. But the earth took to trembling so, they got scared and ran away. Every time he'd ride by the mill after that, something seemed to try to pull Dave off his horse and up toward the spot. But he'd cut his horse a lick and ride clear off the place.

Dave said he'd like to have the money, but not that bad. He never did get it.

By the time the story was over, one of the little boys had found the lost penny in some weeds.

"Hyere's yore penny," they called. "Come rake it out, Jerk-water."

Jerkwater came to with a start. He had moved unconsciously closer and closer to the teller of the ghost story, and his eyes in his freckled face were "biggin' and biggin'," and watching Jerkwater had been almost as good as listening to the story.

Jerkwater would remember that story. And someday he would tell it to somebody who would remember it too.

A Touch of Scarlet

Leyton Hoskins age 72 Apr 1915 ware
farmer and grate lier braggy feler not
much to him

THERE is magic in Appalachia. So may there be
sordidness and sorrow, but the magic is untouchably there. It is
in the high clear air, in the extravagant blueness of the sky if
only for the extravagant moment. The next moment takes care of
itself, if not in blue, then in storm, but using all of itself there is
to use. It's in the summer clouds letting themselves be taken by
the high course of the day, to form and re-form, to dissipate
eventually. What matter? They've had it, they've given it.

And on a suddenly needful return to the North Carolina
mountains for a revival of spirit, I heard about Miss Emma's
giving a touch of magic to the careless love of her youth. Everybody in the village had thought Emma well rid of that no-
account Jim Devon, as braggy a liar as ever drew breath. Everybody except Miss Emma, who was a fair hand at telling a made-
up tale herself.

But there was romantic flare to her imagination, lifting her
head and shoulders above the common run of jilted girls. Hers
was not the hapless plaint of the tender lady made timeless by
ballad warning: "Men are like a star on a cloudy dawn, they'll
first appear, and then they're gone." Emma knew happiness to be
as variable as the seasons; each moment to be taken wholly,
yours not to be held, but to change.

It was on a sunny, easy day with life to it, a just-right day for sauntering, that I heard about the mourning dress she yearned for, and found in the Sales Room of the Crossnore School. Since I used to help unpack the secondhand Sale's amazing miscellany, as did other young teachers then, that part of the story was very believable. The whole of it was put together for me by Crossnore friends of those enchanted days, the lasting sort of friendship that spans time and space. It was told laughingly, which was right too. We were again at shattering war. Miss Emma, the rabbit, and thrifty Mr. Fetty all were like a little bit of quiet in a noisy world.

. . . For the life of him Mr. Fetty could not help but think of a crazy-quilt spread over a feather bed as Miss Emma came easing down the creek-bed road. Ever since she had buried wild Jim Devon in the turnip patch twenty-five years before, she had given no thought to clothes. She was a big woman, and she kept herself covered with vast layers of faded patches.

She looked soft and billowy. And ever since Mr. Fetty's last wife had been laid down in the burying ground, he had thought about Miss Emma a little.

Miss Emma had a gentle face, which her thirty-nine years had loosely folded and creased but left remarkably arbutus-like in coloring and freshness. And her eyes, peering out shyly from under her sunbonnet brim, were only a shade paler than the for-get-me-nots that got themselves helplessly tangled at the creek sides when the water was high.

At the moment there was little water at all in the creek. It was low with summer. Mr. Fetty sat on his porch step and watched her as she came down the creek bed, singing. Her voice was sweet and high and had the same melancholy drift that charac-terized her walk. It just happened she was singing "The sails of my ship are spreading," which was a verse of the one folk song Mr. Fetty knew all the way through. He thought to himself that here was a smart woman, and his heart thumped out the time to the tuneless old song that she knew and he did too.

It was Saturday morning. Mr. Fetty was by no means slack-twisted that he should be sitting on his front porch step in the middle of a Saturday morning. His work-stiffened hands testified to that. He had rolling land almost as far as he could see either way from his old slab house that sat on a foundation of field rock, almost at the edge of the creek bed. He had cash money buried in the apple orchard, a steady eye, and substantial bare feet. The latter he was paddling pleasantly while he waited, in a puddle of warm water left at the bottom of the step by the night's shower of rain.

It was Saturday, and on Saturday Miss Emma came down off the ridge and went to town. He had been waiting to see her go by. Other people had gone by, and he had given them howdy and followed them out of sight around the bend with his impersonally curious gaze.

But there was nothing impersonal in the flashing gaze that jumped up to meet Miss Emma, although the long gaunt man himself continued in his overalled sitting on his rickety porch step. In her turn, Miss Emma was not unaware of his point-blank interest, although she kept her meek gaze carefully on the rocks under her feet, pretending not to see him. Certainly she would have flouted the conscious thought that the light in the eyes going along with her was meaningful. But she could not help knowing it in her heart. No woman could, even though she be bound by an ancient grieving.

When she was squarely in front of him, and so close that out of her eye corners she could see his toes wiggling, he spoke up.

"Mornin', Miss Emma."

Miss Emma came to a stop. Her large shapely hands went through surprisingly effective motions of startledness, while her flabby cheeks knotted up into a peachlike bulk as she smiled shyly.

"Why, Mr. Fetty, I never seen you a-sittin' thar!"

"Been hyere—all mornin'. Goin' to town?"

"Aimin' to."

"La, you women are all of a piece when hit comes to pleasurin' yoreselves by spendin' money." He spat to the side in twice-married assurance and with a masculine indulgence.

Miss Emma lifted her head. He saw how her sweet mild face

under the sunbonnet lit up, how her eyes shone and her thin
lips grew delicately happy. How could he have known how
every thought of hers turned toward Jim just as naturally as
every hollow runs toward the sheltering bosom of a hill, and that
at the moment she was thinking of the mourning dress she was
going to buy in honor of her dead lover—could Mr. Fetty have
known all this, his innards would not have leaped and jumped so.
But in his poor ignorance he imagined it was his tolerant wit that
had so gladdened her. He grinned a bit himself, showing a lack
of some teeth and the good sense that would not allow him to fill
in the gaps with vainglorious gold when soon the whole lot
would go anyway.

Then he fixed her with an earnest eagerness that brought her
out of her transport into an abrupt discomfort. She stood confused under his gaze, and in a secret rise of unnamed pleasure.
She stood looking just past Mr. Fetty, vague and flushed. Mr.
Fetty saw the flush and wriggled his toes deliciously in the sun-
warmed puddle.

It was a delicately balanced silence, with a not-quite touch to
it, and Miss Emma would like to have it go on. But Mr. Fetty
broke it up with a heavy hand.

"Yo're goin' to town reminds me I ought to go myself one of
these days. A lone man gits careless of his clothes. These pants
have come so many holes in 'em I'm about to fall out of 'em."

Miss Emma looked pained and her maidenly spirit backed
away from such rough talk. Still, she kept her place in the
creek bed. With impersonal rebuke, her gaze took refuge in the
disorder of Mr. Fetty's porch. There were two or three ravelty
splint-bottom chairs, a couple of bee gums, strings of dried
pumpkin no longer yellow, and on the house wall hung big
wooden pegs fairly bending down with their loads—clothes stiff
with mud or limp with age, odds and ends of harness, old bas-
kets, and on two of the pegs, in singular honor, homemade hoes.

"My," said Miss Emma brightly, "that porch is shore a sight!"

He screwed around to look, running a brown hand through his
thin sandy hair so that it stood up and fell down like dried corn

leaves left standing on the shock after the fall crop has been har-
vested.

"A man don't know how to do by his lone."

This was even worse than the pants that had come holes in
them. Miss Emma clutched at her scattering composure. A big-
bosomed turkey strutting across the yard reminded her of the
last poor Mrs. Fetty. Then she tried to feel miserable for Mr.
Fetty, but that was hard to do with the bereaved man leaning
forward now, not looking miserable at all but quite excited and
prancy with his brown cheeks reddish and his eyes like a fawn-
ing puppy's. Worse, her own insides were whispering things she
knew well and good she had no right, in loyalty, to listen to.

"Happen someday I'll jest step down and he'p you red things
up," she heard herself offering, which surprised her almost as
much as Mr. Fetty's sudden responding vehemence.

"Miss Emma," he began, and stopped. "Miss Emma," he
swiped his tobacco determinedly around to the other jaw and got
up off the porch step. When he stood up he was too tall, so he
stooped down a little. He leaned his head back toward the first
peg where a hoe was hanging. "Thar," he said, "hangs my first
woman's hoe, and thar," sticking a forefinger at the other, "hangs
my second woman's hoe. How would you like to hang yourn
thar?" he wondered.

He indicated the next peg that scarcely could be seen for the
rotting saddle on it.

For a second Miss Emma thought she was going to faint, she
was so beautifully sick at her stomach. For months now she had
been reasonably sure that Mr. Fetty knew when she went down
the creek and when she came back up, that he watched her with
no disfavor in his gaze. But to have it flung broadside at the wide
world in utter disregard for the listening hills and the gossipy
pines nearabout unsettled her. Her senses scattered here and
yonder and might never have come back had it not been for the
steadiness of his bright eyes drawing them toward the down-go
porch and the cash money in the orchard.

But almost before one could say she actually had faltered,

twenty-five years of faith shoved itself like a ramrod up the plumpness of her weakening back, and she gave her neighbor the ripeness of a wounded but forgiving gaze. Let Mr. Fetty forget his Mrs. Fetty number one and his Mrs. Fetty number two, but she would never forget her Jim!

"Thank you," in gentle pain, "I reckon you meant well enough. But I never could have no heart ease down hyere, with pore Jim a-layin' up yonder in the turnip patch."

Mr. Fetty stood and scratched the end of his thin woebegone nose for a while. Then he dropped himself down again, to dabble his feet in the rain puddle. But it was easily seen there was no more pleasure to be had in that now. He drooped, all the way down, from his long dry locks to his long bony toes. Miss Emma knocked her tongue against her snuff-stained teeth in pity at this forlornness and was very happy. She could think of nothing to say, which was just as well, for not a word could have gotten past the flapping in her throat just then anyway. So she eased on down the creek, her skirts capering discreetly.

Just a piece beyond Mr. Fetty's, the creek met the county road, and from there on she adjusted her wandering stride to wagon ruts, sidetracking half up a bank every while to gather in a handful of the lusciously pouting blackberries growing all along the way. The morning mist had not wholly risen out of the hollows, so that only halves of things were real. There was a pleasant haze to the whole of creation: the sky running back of the pines was like tenderness half known in a dream; even the glazed laurel was kept to a softened mood.

Outwardly, as Miss Emma moved along, she made one with this hush—in her calm set of face and in the fluid, full-bodied softness of her. But inside her there was no hush. The heart that had set its words to sorry tunes and sipped languidly on thin memory for twenty-five years was behaving scandalously—it was prancy and jiggy and working up an appetite for red meat.

"Hit's because I'm a-goin' to git myself a mournin' dress." She said it aloud, in precaution—for she was honestly fearful that the jig in her heart might get into her feet. However, that was unlikely, for her feet were quite big and broad and too used to padding about softly. One of the wonderful things about Devil Jim had been his quick ease of movement, like a mountain cat. His eyes had been quick too. Not just little bitty old ordinary blue eyes like Mr. Fetty's, that told a body something straight out and that was that. But Jim's—Miss Emma reached down into the past to drag out a throbbing uncertainty or two—Jim's had a way of picking her up and throwing her down until she was all in a whirl, with Jim all of her dizziness. And never would he have come flat out and asked, "How would you like yourn to hang thar?" She tossed her head in scorn at this lack of delicacy. But she smiled, and sighed a little, and was cheerful out of all decency.

She left the county road then for a path going up a hill and down through a white-pine thicket and up another rise that was losing its illusion of morning by giving itself over entirely to open sun. From there she could look down on the town, and although no mist lingered there at all and it was quite frankly ugly with its handful of slab structures shying away from the highway, the place bulged with glamor.

On the town side of the hill stood the new school building, big and white, filled with fotched-on teachers and youngins getting onto new ways. As Miss Emma strode by, the children's voices, high and lusty, carried out to her through the open windows of the nearest room. They were singing some highfalutin song she never heard tell of before. Its wide tonal variations fell gratingly on her bonneted ears, trained to the repetitive melody of ballads.

"Humph," she scoffed to herself. "Them painted Jezebels down yonder think they're a-teachin' music."

There was no personal enmity in the opinion. She didn't know a word of a book herself, nor had she any hankering to learn. But in fairness she had to own an obligation to the school, for it had brought in the Rag Shakin', as the community in good-humored slight called the Saturday sale of old clothes and household effects that were sent in to the school from all over the country, to be sold in the school's support.

Miss Emma's high, drifting step became more purposeful on the curving rocky drive that led down from the school into the town squatting in a valley. The highway hurried through it, with a tin café and the old blacksmith shop revised into a filling station standing close on one side trying to stop it; while on the other side was the red general store with the unpainted lean-to post office nudging up against it like a cold bedfellow. Backing off more modestly from the impatient highway was a rock church and the slab Sale Room where the Rag Shakin' was held.

Miss Emma's nostrils dilated with pleasure at sniff of the Saturday stir down there. There were saddle horses and hitched teams, and there were a few automobiles and trucks and more people than ever came to church. Her steps grew longer.

Aunt Betts, who with her husband ran the Rag Shakin', looked out the door and saw her coming.

"Hyere's Emma," she told her husband. "And I've finally got her her dress." Aunt Betts looked glad about it.

"Whar'd hit come from?" asked Uncle Gates. "A tent and awning company?"

"Make fun of her if you want to," retorted his wife coldly.

"I ain't makin' fun of her. And I'm as glad as you are to see her begin to doll herself up. This mournin' around over that no-account Jim Devon has been all foolishness."

"This hyere dress," said his wife, looking him firmly in the eye, "is a mournin' dress for Jim."

Uncle Gates pulled his handlebar mustaches incredulously. "You mean to tell me Emma really believes that yarn of hers about Jim bein' kilt for a rabbit?"

"Hit gives her *appeal*," explained his wife gently. "She's walked in hyere every Saturday since the sale started, a-lookin' for a black dress to mourn him proper in. Thar's never been one come in big enough to cover her front and back both till this week. Hit hain't rightly a dress," she admitted, a little worried, "but hit's black, and I don't want you to open yore fly trap about hit."

"I hain't said a word," protested Uncle Gates. "But hits the craziest thing I ever heard of." Yet he gave Miss Emma a kindly greeting, almost a respectful one.

When Emma had been just a slip of a girl, she and Devil Jim

7   There is something magnificent about
     the old mountain woman.

8   Their high-spirited temperament suggests the sour spiciness of raw-cut pine.

Devon had sat up together. Young Devil Jim came by his nick-
name honestly, but at any word against him Emma's heart had
only beat the harder, and her flaxen head, usually hung low with
timidity, was flung in pride that she should be the choice of wild
Jim Devon. Times, at sound of his free, bold step on the stones
out front, the blood had beaten in her so that she could not see
him clearly, and that was the truth.

But come the wedding day, something happened. Jim was
turned into a rabbit—because Jim disappeared.

But Emma knew that all the witchcraft of the Blue Ridge
could not keep Jim away from her long, for he loved her. And
sure enough, one day soon after, her pap came in home toting a
rabbit by the hind leg. He had said, "Emma, take hit out and
skin hit and we'll have hit for supper. La, that's the tamest critter
ever I seed. Hit was just hoppin' along in front of me, and when
hit come to the gate, hit just sit down, like hit was waitin' for me
to open that gate and let it in. I declar', I hated to shoot hit. But
then, a rabbit's a rabbit!"

Emma had sat down and cried. "That was Jim a-comin' back
to me," she told her pap. "You thought hit was a rabbit, but hit
was Jim." And she didn't skin the rabbit, but she took it out and
buried it in the turnip patch, along with her tears. But not all of
her tears.

Perhaps it was a left-over tear now and then that kept the
shine in her pale eyes as the faithful years went on. Withal, her
grieving was an ornament that became her peculiarly. And although no one really believed the rabbit story, all hill people live
closer to sorrow than to joy, and Miss Emma's adoption of ethe-
real melancholy had indeed, as Aunt Betts had said, given her
appeal.

So Uncle Gates greeted her respectfully as she came up the
slab steps into the crowd. "Livin' good as common, Miss Emma?"
he inquired.

"Tol'able," she granted shyly.

Others turned to look and give her good morning. And although her grayishly flaxen head under the bonnet hung with
meekness, her face was eager and glad of the greetings. It was

pleasant to loiter on the sunny steps to take part in an inconsequent exchange of talk or to stand in silence and spit and listen to the big things going on in the world.

Miss Emma let the better part of an hour go by out there in the sun filling her mind with a rich confusion that she could sort out at leisure during the rest of her lone week. Then she went inside.

The simple one-room structure was lined with rough shelves and a broad counter, both piled high with almost anything: corsets, curtains, slightly used toothbrushes, old shoes and new ones, zippered dresses and bustled ones, furs and family photographs; a bag of buttons, a Boy Scout cooking kit, a sack of peach seeds, and a man's ham-smacker suit—all eventually salable. Hanging back of the counter in inviting prominence were a lavender lace evening gown, a brown wig, and an ear trumpet. At the rear of the store, tacked up on a post, was a motto that also had come out of somebody's attic: "CHEER UP, IT MIGHT BE WORSE."

Miss Emma looked around her admiringly, in never-failing fresh wonder, and thought what a fine world it must be yon side the hills.

"How you, Emma?" called Aunt Betts.

"Fine," sang Miss Emma "what there is of me." And they both laughed a little.

"Yore dress come." And Aunt Betts beckoned to her mysteriously.

Miss Emma's heart gave a frightened leap and her face began doing lovely things because of an inward light. Trembling, she made her way around a woman with a crying baby and two old men fighting the war. "Why," said one importantly, "we got troops all over creation." But for Miss Emma the world had grown suddenly small—no bigger than her heart. She stood, clasping and unclasping her hands, afraid to ask. But Aunt Betts nodded.

"Silk, too. Right straight from China. Come on back behind the counter and we'll go in t'other room. I got hit put away for you in thar. Hit hain't just exactly a dress, though," she warned.

"Hit's more a wrapper. And hit's got just the least tech of scarlet of hit."

But it was only scarlet trimmed, and when Aunt Betts handed her the suit box with the black Chinese kimono lying folded in it, Miss Emma stood a minute, looking at it as though someone from the out and beyond had wrapped up all that was worth living for and sent it to her.

"Hit'll fit you," promised Aunt Betts. "Hit's big. And hit's good," she added. "Hit'll cost you a dollar and a half."

Miss Emma did not trust herself to speak. With shaking fingers she reached deep inside her patched blouse and brought forth a small patched bag full of bills. It yielded the dollar, and from another little bundle halfway up a petticoat came the change. Miss Emma was pale, as if on her wedding day. She felt a great need to be alone.

"Try hit on if you want to," said Aunt Betts, and seemed a little relieved to get back into the store with its crowd of faces she could understand.

Left alone in the sanctuary of the narrow storage room, Miss Emma leaned back against a rack of winter coats and closed her eyes. Her hands were clutching the cool silk kimono into wrinkles. Her expression wore saintly robes, and within her was a rapture beside which the loose joy caused by her recent encounter with Mr. Fetty seemed crass.

Then she opened her eyes and held the kimono up to her, smoothed it and patted it. Finally she got modestly behind a barrel, peeled to her top petticoat, and put the kimono on. It was as soft as she was, with a wide scarlet sash that wrapped her around the middle and with the low-cut scarlet-bound neck startling the creaminess of her throat.

"La," murmured Miss Emma. "La!"

She stayed in the back room for a good little piece, viewing her dress. She regretted the touch of scarlet. But as she ran her fingers over the greater bulk of black, she scraped her soul again through the ecstasy—the exquisite anguish—of love unconsummated, enriched by twenty-some years of mellowing embellishment.

And then, slowly, she began knowing a strange thing. The embellishment was all there was left. Even as she stood smoothing her mourning bosom, all emotion about Jim, even all interest, died. She grew quite still, to feel it go. . . .

Mr. Fetty did not look as she came along. He was busy taking tomatoes out of a big worn basket and laying them up on bee gums to ripen. Miss Emma stopped.

"Mr. Fetty . . ." she said.

"I been a-studyin'," said Mr. Fetty, laying up another tomato. "And I'm about decided to raise fightin' cocks instead of botherin' with another woman."

He stood up independently. Then his mouth dropped. He got goose pimples. Miss Emma was doing something to him neither his first wife had, nor his second. She was giving him the jim jams. Mr. Fetty stood straight, his eyes bright on her.

"Hit's my mournin' dress," explained Miss Emma with sweet melancholy of the black kimono with its touch of scarlet. "I've done wore hit for one man a'ready. How'd you like to be the next one to have it wore for, Mr. Fetty?"

Edge of Damnation

Steven buckanen age 70 June 5 1898 he war preacher baptis

IT had rained in the night, and although it was sunny afternoon now, there still was that lush giveableness to the earth —the smell of green things growing and the rank health of roots faintly mingled with the smell of muddy boots and the dim sweetness of snuff, and of people. It had turned out to be a fine day and the mountain church was crowded.

It was small and simple, of raw new plank. It belonged to the congregation in the way anything does that you work with personally. Someone had given the land, others had given their time to clear it—although laurel and oak and pine were still familiarly close. Some of the men apt with carpentry tools had tithed their labor and built the building and made the plank pews that lined up on either side of the center aisle. Out by the front steps was a pile of poplar bark that had been cut into shingles and weighed down with rocks to shape and season. It would be some months before those finishing shingles would be ready to put on and there was no glass in the windows as yet. "Window lights" cost cash money, and that was slow to accumulate. So the windows were just openings. The fresh smell of the woods was full in the little room, and a blackberry twig leaned in from the outside over the front window hole. Every time Uncle Joe, who was preaching, got particularly "tempestuous" and paced the raw plank platform the while he "delivered himself with great liberty," that blackberry twig would wag impudently.

But if the blackberry twig was impudent, it was the only thing in the little mountain church that was. Even the babes in arms were hushed as their mothers swayed back and forth to the ominous rhythm of Uncle Joe's eloquence.

Uncle Joe was just a little man, in little gold-rimmed spectacles. But he was mighty. He had an oratorical gift any public speaker might well envy. He had begun his sermon with a commanding hush of expectation that gradually swept up to thunder —only to stop, abruptly, leaving us hanging. Then he picked us up and started over.

Uncle Joe was of the vanishing order of "home-grown" mountain preachers, and one of the few requisites of the regime was that a man of God have "good wind." Uncle Joe did pretty well. This Sunday he had begun with Genesis and gone right straight through to Revelations, with never a pause except for dramatic effect. To be exact about such a span, however, it must be said he hit only the violent high spots. The slender thread of goodness that runs with surprising strength, considering its slimness, through the account, he ignored. But he dwelt masterfully on those sections dealing with the everlasting fires. For three solid hours that Sunday evening I sat, fascinated, on the brittle edge of damnation.

It really was in the middle of the afternoon. But for the southern mountain people "evening" begins at twelve o'clock noon. For them the morning and the evening are the day, as it is recounted in Genesis of a world still in the making.

As the sermon went on, I began to feel a little surer of Uncle Joe's wind than I did of his Scripture. He had a way of throwing in his wife Martha's remarks along with those of the Prophets. But it was interesting. At the end I especially remember the way his wife Martha and Ezekiel got together on perdition for the young and frivolous.

"As my wife Marthy says," threatened Uncle Joe—beginning softly on the "wife," then using all his breath on "Marthy" so that the "says" was somewhat like exhaustion although, after all, the whole phrase got saved by a last-instant staccato catch upward that gave him a fresh start again—"you young folks are a-goin' to be roasted, ah. Yo're a-goin' to be laid out on the coolin' board only to burn ag'in, ah—as Ezekiel says, ah, yo're a-goin' to all be cast down into Hell, ah." (The aspirate "ah" gives the holy tone.)

Suddenly, moved himself by the completeness of the prospect he was presenting, he stepped to the very edge of the platform, leaned down toward the front row of us staring up at him, and shook a grubby forefinger so close under our noses he almost scratched them, while he gave out his final word on doom.

"A double L," he sang out in solemn pronouncement, "spells ALL ends ALL and kivers ALL!"

Then he straightened from that last downward swoop and grimly lined out a hymn. Everybody got silently to his feet and sang. The men carried the bass and the women swung in and out on it in nasal wails. At the song's end everybody turned meekly and started to file out. But the stern little theologian stepped down off the pulpit and held up a detaining hand.

"Wait a minute. Young Jim Archer up the branch has fell out of a wagon bed and sprung his back. He can't neither walk nor set. Hit's a-comin' on another windin', rainin' spell, and Joe ain't got his 'taters in yet. Now, how many of you folks are a-goin' to meet up at Joe's place tomorrow to help git his 'taters in fer him?"

Uncle Joe is a fair example of the old-type mountain preachers who preached a harsh and narrow doctrine often quite at variance with their real humanity. In their capacity of spiritual leadership, the better of them came not only into a firm hold on the deeper things of life, but into a sympathy and understanding with their fellows as well. They were peculiarly equipped for an understanding of the particular problems of their charge, for six days a week they lived through the same trials and experiences. For six days a week the "home-grown" preacher tilled his rocky fields just as his neighbor did; or he made wagons, or bottomed chairs, or cobbled shoes, or shoed horses, or made teeth.

Dentistry as a means of making a living for the cloth came to me a startled first time in an overheard bit of conversation. In a small Kentucky hill town, two sunbonneted women had stopped to pass the time of day. One was sitting on the seat of a jolt wagon and the other had a big hickory basket of eggs she'd brought to town to sell. She also had some new teeth, it seemed, from the other's interested observation and admiration.

"I declare, that's the purtiest set of teeth I ever seen in anybody's head! La, don't they shine in the sun!"

"Preacher Goudy made 'em for me," said their owner modestly.

Occasionally, in the mountains as anywhere else, there was to be found a minister whose business sense was perhaps a little clearer than his concept of his divine calling. A preacher who played one of the side roles in the famous Hatfield-McCoy feud, for instance, sold the liquor that was often the cause of renewed trouble, sold the arms that made it active, used the shipping crates the guns had come in to make the necessary coffins, and then collected a fee for the funerals he preached.

For the most part, however, these self-made ministers were earnest in the giving of themselves—poring over the Scriptures by the light of a smoky lamp after their weekday's work was done, and then waiting in faith for the "speerit" to give them utterance on the seventh day.

The prevailing religion of the southern mountains is Protestantism, naturally, since the beginning of colonization there had its source in the second great Protestant migration of English-speaking people to the New World. The first such migration had occurred about a hundred years before, when the Pilgrims landed at Plymouth Rock. Up to a certain point the two histories are very similar—that of a group of people with an inspired, resolute urge. The parallel stops with the entrance of the second group to that new land.

From odd bits of written sources you can string together the rest of the story. And occasionally you can find someone among the mountain people themselves to tell it. I heard a colloquial but very sound expression of it in a country valley in West Virginia. Like so many such hill communities, it still is back in time although it is only a little way from the main highway. I sat on the porch of a log cabin in which that part of West Virginia had first cast its vote for the black abolitionist, Lincoln. My host was a shrewd, keen back-country doctor, and the cabin has been his office for a long time. He is quite a student and has a good deal of scorn for what he has learned.

"Why," he told me in disgust, "our country was first settled by people comin' over here to escape religious persecution, but they hadn't any more than got their pants warmed till they were meetin' the newcomers with the very same kind of persecution!"

He was referring particularly to that group of Scotch-Irish and English immigrants from the Covenanting Wars who landed on American shores only to find here, too, religious and political persecution—this time in the form of Parliament levying what they considered undue taxes and insisting upon a state church. But the stubborn Scotch-Irish Presbyterians persisted in building their own meetinghouses. They grew into a force to be considered, and by 1700 their ministers were being granted the right to preach. But still they were harassed by the Established Church and kept pushing on westward toward some place of their own, which came to be, finally, the magnificent wilderness of the mountains.

But once entered, that wilderness closed behind them and they were cut off from the rest of the world. With that separation went gradually one of the chief characteristics of the great stream of early Protestant migration. High intellectual standards were essential to the survival of the strong independent force that had turned them from old European oppression to new times. And early records do show that in their first settlements in this country, beside every church a school was built. But as they went on into the wilderness, pioneer conditions discouraged the continuance of those standards.

Men with learning who might have taught their children needed all their time to clear the land and make a shelter, break ground for their fields, hunt down meat, and protect the new-made home from the attacks of the Indians. The women, too, had more to occupy them than sitting down with books. They had brought with them into the wilderness a colonial civilization. But the colonial civilization did not include the common school.

Thus the mountain preachers, as the generations went away

backward into their strange and unforeseen isolation, came to have little or no education. Sometimes this lack carried all the laughableness, and the danger, of utter ignorance—as in the mountain preacher who declared with pious pride, "I'm jest a pore ignorant man, ah, and I pray God, ah, that He'll make me ten times more ignoranter, ah"—which was a good deal to ask. But just as often, the "home-grown" mountain preacher kept a native sageness that, if it did not compensate for the lack of learning, at least tided it over.

Across a wild part of the Tennessee border from Uncle Joe's church there was another little one, manned by a mountain preacher. He was a bachelor—a raw-cut man with a big nose that twitched when he laughed, with his thin upper lip marking the strength of his mouth and the full lower one giving it humanness—and a practical sort. Somehow you went out from his church, with its lamp-lit shadows of people, feeling that the whole earth was quiet and at rest.

It was his unique closing service that gave this feeling. It was homely, direct, and friendly; in a way one of the congregation put it, sincerely and with the naturalness that lets mountain people voice unself-consciously whatever good they feel: "It's Godamighty in the hearts of folks that makes friendship."

After "all minds had been discharged and the benediction craved," the congregation stayed on a few moments while the minister called the Lord's attention to the individual needs and personal reasons for thanksgiving of each and every member. If "Sister Campbell was tired of burning her brains out bending over a stove that het too hot," then the Lord was asked to see what could be done about persuading her husband—who had made some money in his time and still had all of it—to buy her a new one. If some brethren not so regular in church attendance as might be had got down sick and was up again, then prodding thanks were given that he had been spared to come back to meeting.

When the preacher found that a young widow of the congregation was out of firewood, he prayed that the Almighty would put it into the minds of her neighbors to get together and give her a wood-chopping. The neighbors responded so well that it was the best wood-chopping the country had ever seen. They chopped the young widow enough wood to last a whole year. And when the preacher married her the next day, what was there to do, after thinking it over, but admire him?

That he was sincerely benign, as well as a good planner, was evidenced in the way he included perfect strangers in his concern. One night, after he had made the rounds of his little flock, he opened his eyes and peered carefully around to make sure none had been overlooked. His survey came to a pause with the back seat. A vacationer from the North who had come to play golf at Linville was with us that night. He was a stranger to the preacher, with his particular wants, hopes, and fortunes unknown. But after a contemplative moment the preacher again lowered his great head, closed his eyes, and did what he could in the way of presentation.

"Lord," he said simply, "bless the stranger in our midst, I can't rightly call You his name, but by the cut of his pants he's an outlander."

Since one of the strong traits of highlanders is individualism, it is but natural that religion, too, should get its personal interpretation. There is an occasional preacher (he preaches around when they're short on preachers) in the Wind Ridge area who gives so very free a translation of the Scriptures that I could not help telling him so. His gray eyes merely looked at me and through me and into a dispassionate past, and he said calmly:

"It's been translated several times before. I feel free to give it another. Look at King James's men—they sat around and voted on what was to come in and what to go out, just like a political convention."

According to his particular version, "The Lord started out to be a God of Love. But pretty soon His creatures got so ornery on His hands, He had to swipe 'em all out and start over again with Noah, who followed the trade of the sea. But it wasn't any time at all before things were gittin' bad again. So He sent Moses up on a mountain to open up a stone quarry and write down a whole new set of laws. But my soul alive, Moses didn't even any more'n get down off that mountain with his new stoneware under his arms till the people were breakin' those laws!"

All in all, his narrow-eyed, unillusioned look-back over the generations that have made not too much progress in the way of human behavior seemed to offer little hope for the future. But when he was questioned on this point, he grew quite earnest. He pulled at his right ear lobe consideringly and granted, "It's a mystery, that perversity of the human family. But," he insisted, "the Lord started out to be a God of Love, and I'll lay to it, that He's goin' to go ahead and see that idea through, just to prove it! Love," treating it thoughtfully, searchingly, "that's the touchstone. That's the magnet. 'Love the Lord thy God with all thy heart'; 'Love thy neighbor as thyself' and—" he finished practically—"keep your chin up even though your spirits are low."

Religion always has been a favorite topic of discussion with the mountain people, and evidently a matter of much musing thought—although often within the limitations of thought without learning.

But perhaps the very mountain boundaries that stranded those first searchers of stubborn courage, in the strange ways of compensation may have kept that originally inspired urge alive. Differently, but offering something not there before.

If they had been stranded in the middle of ugliness, the spirit might well have dwindled and dwarfed with the going of knowledge. But when the spirit is world-heavy, weighed down with all the mistakes and confusions and sorrows and humiliations that can come in the frail time of humans, it is like promise to stand in a morning when the near hills are dark with the feel of rain but, away off, the far ones are in a lighted mist. It is beautiful and good over there, and clean and simple. It is more positive than solace. The very promise that the heart can be light again lets you turn and go onward toward fulfillment.

The War Amongst Us

Dave Oakes age 40 dide apr 5 1862
shot by John Parmer in war

"WAR is the beastiality of man," mused an Appalachian sage whose eyes looked back to see the present. "And," he added dryly, "I reckon my folks have been in every war and dogfight this country's ever had."

Since their American beginnings, whether they lived in scattered settlements or in the fastness of lonely forest, the frontiersmen had come together in war—a mighty force in the freedom and growth of their country. And in the Civil War, the southern mountain people bespoke a nation ripped asunder.

The highlanders have a very personal name for the War of the Rebellion, as it is listed in Official Records. With their aptness for the descriptive phase, they call it the War Amongst Us. And with irony befitting that tragedy of human errors, it was one of their own, the Kentucky-born man of sorrows, Abraham Lincoln, who broke their unity.

In the spring of 1861, when Lincoln gave the call to arms, again the mountain men responded, but with a difference. For the first time in their long annals of unwavering patriotism, their force was divided.

The contention was not over slavery. On the whole, these independents of the earth were a group of landowners, not slaveholders. The rugged individualists who fought under the Stars and Stripes held to their fiery belief in the Union their forefathers had helped create. Those who fought under the Stars and

Bars held to their fiery belief in individual State's Rights, as guaranteed by the United States Constitution. And as always, there was the ilk on both sides that a seasoned highlander remembered hearing said about a neighbor up the creek. "He was so danged patriotic he sacrificed every one of his wife's relatives to gain victory."

Where the black of a mountain can climb to a height with nothing gentle in its aspect, ridged and seared and worn to bare rock in places, one North Carolina county was cracked so squarely across the middle by seething sentiment, it broke completely in two. In the county dominated by Southern conviction, the property of Northerners was outrageously overtaxed. Self-constituted authorities justified the galling action as a war measure.

In the county where ardent Northern sentiment prevailed, only those families loyal to the Union were allowed to buy salt. When a customer known to favor the Rebellion ventured into a settlement store, the storekeeper would say blandly, by way of unyielding refusal, "Lots of folks are a-hurtin' for salt." The smackless taste of food without salt could be endured, but this was cattle country, and cattle sickened without that essential ingredient.

At the war's excitable beginning, from the abrupt uprising of the Virginia Blue Ridge to the green hills of Alabama and Georgia, men hurried to the nearest recruiting center. Both North and South confidently expected the "trouble" to be over in a few months.

In the extreme northwest hills of Virginia, the Ohio River town of Wheeling, because of its thriving north-south river traffic, boasted a Government Customs House. By May of 1861, the Customs House was doing a lively traffic in recruiting men for the Federal army.

The initial lot of enthusiasts, feeling that *they* represented the real spirit of Sovereign Virginia, called themselves The First Regiment of Virginia. With the Confederates also trying to woo the men of the northwest, the title was so dubious that Lincoln's War Department hesitated about issuing regulation equipment.

So the First Regiment drilled sans uniform. Their arms were sup-
plied by private citizens.

At the same time, although Wheeling was predominantly
Northern in sympathy, a private citizen of Southern persuasion
outfitted the Shriver Grays. Their uniforms were made by his
cautious tailor, at night, in an upstairs shop behind locked doors.

The budding soldiers themselves, however, had played together, gone fishing or courting together; so, in high good
spirits, they drilled cooperatively on the town's two parallel, and
comparatively level, streets. The Northern boys marched down
Market Street while the Southern boys marched up Main Street
—virtually chasing each other.

Meanwhile, the little down-state town of Clarksburg, by dint
of its central location in that mountainous section, boasted a
United States Armory. The Northern boys drilled in the armory
on Monday, Tuesday, and Wednesday. The Southern boys drilled
there on Thursday, Friday, and Saturday. On Sunday nobody
drilled.

Action came on a stormy midnight in early June. The nearby
village of Phillipi, entered from the north by a wooden covered
bridge and at that time a Confederate training camp, sent
alarmed word of imminent attack. Since contestants weren't quite
ready yet to kill one another on sight, the Northern boys gave
their Southern friends and relations a head start. The Southern-
ers ran so fast they crossed the rattling bridge in time to join the
encampment's dawn stampede down the muddy road heading
south. Thus the first engagement of the Civil War is historically
known as the Phillipi Races—a tag name that the humiliated
young Rebels grimly resolved to change. And they valiantly did,
fighting and dying with gay courage.

Not all young students who dropped their schoolbooks to pick
up muskets got that far with their soldiering. In one hilltown
family the sons went different ways. The younger boy, with
scarcely a sign of fuzz on his cheeks, finding himself encamped
near home, slipped through the picket lines. It was an unsol-
dierly thing to do, but he was hungry for some of his mother's
fresh-baked bread. Instead of Mother welcoming him with open

arms when he walked jauntily in the front door, she was dismayed. Upstairs, her other son, home on furlough, was preparing to return to his Federal company. Being a quick-witted woman, she hustled her young miscreant into the back pantry. But like a fool, he left his cap behind. The older brother, perfectly within his rights as a Union officer on pro-Northern grounds, had the disgusted kid arrested and put in jail for safe-keeping.

Except for the Baltimore and Ohio Railroad, which had laid its last arduous track through the mountains to its Wheeling terminus a scant decade before, so little had been known about the southern Appalachian range, it was generally considered an impregnable barrier to easy communication between the established Atlantic coast and the growing West. The topographical significance of the mountains that rolled and tumbled and heaved up in peaks, cutting through the vitals of eight southern states, dawned for the first time on a nation at war within. Then it became desperately important to both North and South to hold that border fastness and its precarious passes.

Consequently, highland farms cleared laboriously out of forests were turned into skirmish grounds for foraging soldiers, officially living off the land and unofficially looting.

A Yankee war correspondent following McClellan's army around Virginia in May of 1862 was a reporter of unusual candor. From the shadow of Slaughter Mountain he wrote an eyewitness account of what he considered "a very serious state of facts." In his opinion, the Federal army was making "rapid strides toward villainy. Men who at home would shudder to touch another's property now remorselessly appropriate whatever comes in reach. I blush to state that on the march I have seen our soldiers rush in crowds upon a farm and quarrel with each other to get the best share of provisions, horses, equipment, with unscrupulous disregard to the protest or condition of the owners. In innumerable instances, families incapable of sustaining the slightest loss, actually have been deprived of all."

You can still hear that report in echoed essence all through the mountains, although there you hear both sides of the story. And the very brushing past of the words "Civil War" can bring memory in a rush. Only last spring an attractive and able young lawyer, her eyes flashing, told me that her home town of Romney, just a hamlet in eastern West Virginia, between 1861 and 1865, had been taken and retaken fifty-six times! Not that she was there during those besieged days. But she did remember, laughing a little, how prickly the wreaths felt that the school children were made to carry to the cemetery every spring in honor of the town's heroic dead "who fell in defense of Southern rights."

The struggle for possession of the northernmost of the southern states, borderline Virginia, was bound to be agonizingly acute. Moreover, it was divided within itself. In Virginia's western roughs there was enough vigorously active Union sentiment to secede from the governing control of tidewater Richmond, the hastily established capital of the Confederacy. And in the cold middle of the war Lincoln acknowledged the state born of strife. In a telegram sent to the temporary capital at Wheeling— housed in Linsley Military Academy—the President gave West Virginia to the nation as a New Year's present.

And it was in the deeply wooded and cliff-broken Virginia mountains that Stonewall Jackson introduced his maxim for warfare, that where two men can walk, an army can go. But the Confederate General's maxim also proved devastating in other sections of Appalachia, in varying ways and degrees.

"Nary a place was safe the minute either of them armies come in sight," said a man who lived above the Big Falls of Elk near the Tennessee border. "They'd rob the hen roosts, smokehouses, break into springhouses to get the milk and butter. And whichever outfit of varmints stepped over a doorstone they'd fair gut a dwellin' house—strip the beds, take clothes, pots and kettles, even frumpery they hadn't an earthly use for. But the hatefulest lot of fiesty scoundrels were the raiders, North and South both. They'd take the harness and gear from the barns, to say nothin' of all the livestock they could lay hand to, anything that could travel or they didn't butcher in the yard, usin' fence rails for kindlin'."

The war had its effect on mountain commerce too, such as it was. Cash money never had been plentiful in Appalachia. Business traditionally was conducted by the barter system. The method ranged from a country woman bringing a dozen eggs into a village store in exchange for "a dustin' of sugar" to a real-estate transaction made by Coleman Hobson, who traded half of Hump Mountain above Cranberry, North Carolina, for two wagon wheels and a shotgun.

By summer of 1863, prices were skyrocketing and the value of the dollar was dropping accordingly. At the outset, highland storekeepers of occupied towns welcomed the free-spending soldiers, until they mournfully discovered that they were being paid, if paid at all, in Secesh bills or in the almost equally worthless Philadelphia banknotes flooding the country. And the evil days were drawing nigh when the countryside customers had so little with which to barter that hungry children did not laugh so often. The once young and vibrant women, waiting to rise up to meet tragedy, began feeling a sifting gray weariness through their very bones as they skimped and scraped to keep their brood's bodies and souls together.

It had been a freshly green and blooming April when the soldiers left their hills, with a faintly acid tang to the white bloom of the wild thorn. Then, on a spring day four years later, the wild bloom fell. An April wind took it, so that its white fall was oddly swift and direct. On Virginia's down-country field of Appomattox, the gentlemanly Lee surrendered the Confederate army to General Ulysses Grant. For the remnant of highland soldiers who straggled home, the safe and wounded with keepsakes of fallen comrades, the ending of this war was as its beginning. There had been none like it.

Mountain men had returned from other wars. Not only had the backwoodsmen come thundering home from stopping the inland march of the King's Redcoats, but enough of their incomparable riflemen had gone to George Washington's aid along the Potomac to be mustered in as the First Foot Regiment of the Continental Army. They had come back from the Indian wars that opened up for settlement Georgia and Alabama and Spanish

Florida. Some had returned from as far away as Mexico. Mountaineer veterans were not altogether proud of their country's aggressive invasion of Mexico, especially after seeing the disputed territory thus gained: Texas. As one green-hills farmer noted critically, finding it a long way home through all that flat sand and sagebrush, "The ground's not fit, scarcely, to raise nothin' but Hell on."

Always, wherever they had been, their strong blue mountains, in a stormy twilight with a promise of sun, had drawn them back. Never before had they returned to find their own loved homeland invaded by war's waste.

A Northern correspondent for *Blackwood's Magazine*, shocked into impartiality by what he had seen of the desolation wrought by the foot soldiers and mounted raiders who crossed and recrossed the ragged range, wrote starkly: "The land was green when they came. They left it a desert."

Not quite. The correspondent did not take into account the mettle of the mountain people—a high-spirited temperament suggestive of the sour spiciness of raw-cut pine. Neither flame nor sword nor the pounding of marauding hoofs could totally destroy their land. Ownership of property gave a man stature. And something more.

If you have ever picked up an ordinary piece of rough mountain field stone, its sharp edge like a hurt to the heart, love of that high land grows understandable. The stone may look cold gray, until you turn it to the light and see the sparkling bits of crystal buried in deep. Its roughness does not smooth, nor its hardness gentle. But it warms to the hold—it fits; consoling, sure, and, for the moment, clung to.

Victors and vanquished alike, the homecoming soldiers still had not only their land but an obdurate courage, and frontier ingenuity. "Perhaps nowhere else on the continent are there such treasures of natural power as are buried in the genuine rural mountaineer. He rarely loses his self-possession, his native intellect and sagacity are extraordinary and susceptible to high development under the proper direction or the stimulus of ambition." This estimation, taken from an 1870 *West Virginia Hand Book and Immigrant Guide*, might have changed the whole course of Appalachian history had proper direction been forthcoming from the outside.

As it was, their unexpectedly strong show of Union loyalty had roused the enmity of the Southern States, which had taken the support of their mountain counties for granted—a resentment that lingered on in lowland indifference to upland needs. The national government, in the engrossed throes of re-establishing itself as a central power, failed to recognize the invaluable loyalty of its highland soldiers, or the potential worth of its self-reliant Appalachian citizens.

So once again the mountain people withdrew into the isolation that imperceptibly had been closing in long before the man-made trouble. But this time they withdrew proudly, to mend the damage as best they could. It never would have crossed their minds to ask for help, or accept it, unless it were offered as one neighbor to another—a favor to be returned.

As their isolation deepened in the aftermath of the Civil War, racial traits, already grown distinctive through their generations as a separate people, intensified, for good and ill. That sense of belonging to a place can be a staying thing in its quiet rightness, and in sanguine instances it stayed—a benefit to all things else. However, only the most sensational news about the again forgotten people reached to the outside world, where the eastern seaboard basked in comfortable commerce and the smokestacks of industry rose prosperously to the west. The violence of the blood feuds (most of them with their origin in the War Amongst Us) especially was prime headline material at the turn of the century.

And well into this century the Appalachian highway system remained about the way it was testily described in a dispatch during the civil strife. "I encountered, aside from rheumatic pains, such roads as no intelligent gray mare of domestic habits ever encountered before. It seems as though all the men, women, and children of this district had spent the leisure hours of their entire existence rolling huge stones down from the mountains onto the roads."

It was true that the highlanders were not entirely blameless.

Some were in no hurry to improve their roads that tended to "ford the creek endwise" for the benefit of curious furriners and lowland officials. As late as 1911, a native and far-seeing North Carolina owner and operator of mica mines that eventually extended from Uncle Jake Carpenter's Three Mile Creek neighborhood to Georgia, still had to haul his ore down off the Blue Ridge to the railroad in wagons drawn by oxen.

But good roads are more than a means of transportation. They are a way to the meeting of minds and a quickening exchange of ideas. By the 1930's, the National Park Service was starting its superlatively researched work of building scenic routes through the magnificent forests of the Great Smokies and the Blue Ridge, thus opening to all Americans the mysterious beauty of the mountains. Even then an old Tennessee man took a wary view of this mark of progress, saying with nostalgic regret, "In this day and time, it's hard to find folks that aren't a-runnin' too fast." Actually, there are still back-country dirt and creek-bed roads aplenty, and communities little touched by progress.

People everywhere take unto themselves something of their natural surroundings. And something of the quality of their mountains is deep in the Appalachian ethnic character—a frontier civilization that never again will appear on earth, not always admirable but seldom dull, kept for a little while yet by the great American Civil War—perhaps for a time when it may be refreshingly needed.

Somewhere in the Greenbrier country, over measureless miles of spectacular mountains, there is a community I'd heard referred to as Wild Run. Recently a young man of lithe ease, who hailed from there, courteously corrected me. Its real name, he explained, was Baptist Church Run Southern Branch Unincorporated. It was only called Wild Run, he said with a slight smile, because of the nature of its people.

If Name Be Needed

*Joseph Carpenter age 18 dide aug 16
1862 he fot for his contery like good
solder and loste lif*

SOME things are known immediately. Some things known immediately still take time to realize fully. So it is with the role played by our southern mountain people in the Civil War.

In the immediate clamor of that dramatic strife, it is doubtful if a confused Washington knew exactly how indebted it was to the startling number of men who emerged from their high wilds and joined the Federal army. It would take time for valid records to show that a hundred thousand Appalachian volunteers, and probably scores not on the muster rolls, responded to Lincoln's 1861 call to arms; that one typical county in the thinly populated Kentucky mountains was stripped of every man and boy from fifteen to sixty; that the Governor of South Carolina complained in a letter to a Confederate friend about the troublesome active Union sentiment in the upland counties; that as far south as Alabama men were leaving their fertile green hills for northern enlistment centers. All up and down the range, the long hunters from the hills might have been hazy about military regulations, but their nonchalant frontier skill with a rifle, their lean endurance, were decided Federal assets as the war dragged on. All were sons of a fighting race, untaught to fail.

Fewer in numbers but no less endowed with a reckless, if not always disciplined courage, were the mountaineers who cast their lot with the Confederates. And there were enough young Rebels among them, all under twenty-four, to make up one third of the fast-moving, fast-striking "foot cavalry" of the Stonewall Brigade.

Although the French government did not come to the aid of the South, as continually expected, in early autumn of 1862, Napoleon's nephew personally crossed the ocean to pay his respects to the Confederate General whose daring exploits were beginning to thrill half of Europe. To his surprise, he found the elusive Stonewall, rightly rumored to be the idol of the South and the terror of the North, a simple-appearing man—and his little army looking more like a rakish band of Falstaff's followers than regimental soldiers infused with the dauntless spirit of their leader. All in all, the Count was so impressed that upon his return to France he had medals made for each brigadier. The shipment got sidetracked in a tin waterfront warehouse and was discovered, rusted by the years, too late.

As for our own government, if it ever appreciated the noteworthy and lasting service of its loyal highlanders in saving the Union, the obligation went unacknowledged. The very flag that flew victoriously from the battletop of Tennessee's Lookout Mountain would have gone without even limited honor, in the obscurity of the standard-bearer's cabin, had it not been rescued by a schoolteacher.

By similar token, in many a modest hilltown home you can still find the Confederate flag occupying the old-time place of honor, above a modern living-room fireplace. Occasionally it is the actual tattered and torn banner borne valorously off the field. More often it is only a colored lithograph of the Stars and Bars, brightly whole. In either case, the emblem of a cause loved and lost is safeguarded by the crystalline silence of glass—not to be touched, but there.

Over a hundred years have gone by since the Civil War. For the ordinary mountaineer no popular songs or poems have been written, no public statues erected, to commemorate either their contributions or their losses in that deeply divisive fray.

If name be needed for the countless thousands of unsung descendants of God-fearing, determined pioneers in a war that divided a nation and its families, Stonewall Jackson names them all. True, his world-wide renown is unique. Yet, for all that, he shared the ordinary highland background.

In his letters to his sister Laura in western Virginia, where he had been born and fostered, he happily called the wooded hills that were his home until he was seventeen "my native land." And he frequently returned. Of Scotch-Irish and English ancestry, he evidenced a temperament germane to the transplanted American highlanders—even to unpredictable, sometimes maddening behavior. And he shared the common highland fate in that his, too, was the proverbial house divided.

During his last term of teaching at the Virginia Military Institute, he expressed an invincible opinion to Laura's teen-age son Thomas. "I am in favor of making a thorough trial for peace, but if we fail in this and Virginia is invaded, to defend it with terrific resistance." The letter to his namesake, whom he would never see again, ended on a note of portent. "People who are anxious for war don't know what they are bargaining for; they don't know the horrors that must accompany such an event."

His last letter to Laura, dated Lexington, Virginia, April 6, 1861, was in answer to one from her, written when she was in the depths of personal discouragement. Hearteningly, her older brother wrote her from experience: "When a cloud comes between you and the sun, do you fear it will never shine again? Pray for more faith."

Then, abruptly, with the opening of hostilities, all communication between the brother and only sister who had kept devotedly close since their orphaned childhood broke off, never to be resumed. Laura exerted her native intelligence and warm womanly efforts toward wresting her western mountain country free from Old Virginia. And something of the rugged hills and clear waters of his youth rode with the Confederate General as he led his handful of men against a host to victory after confounding victory, his right hand raised mysteriously to heaven.

Several years ago, when the light of spring lay on the hills, I was a guest in the home of Stonewall's namesake, Thomas Jackson Arnold, a sweet and gallant gentleman. At the time, he was living in the same West Virginia vicinity that had produced his illustrious uncle. During the course of my visit, most generously and with his blessing, my host gave me a copy of a priceless diary, written when his Uncle Thomas was twelve.

It was not written by young Thomas, but by a companion in adventure. Since nobody had the dreamiest notion that the poor, not overly quick-witted country boy was destined to be great among men, the diary is refreshingly uncluttered by the awe of later biographers. Yet all unwittingly, the youthful scribe gives a vibrant word sketch of his friend and life in his times that presages the future. Merely as an account of a couple of boys taking a venturesome horseback trip, with a natural interest in everything along the way, it is a delight entitled:

DIARY OF A JOURNEY TO PARKERSBURG, 1841,
BY THOMAS JACKSON AND MYSELF.

"Sunday Thom came down from the Jackson's mill to Clarksburg and put up at his Aunt Katey's. He brought two horses, one for himself and one for me, to ride to Parkersburg to meet the ship from Pittsburgh and bring back a small piece to repair the mill machinery for his Uncle Cummins. At early candlelight we went again to church. Thom says he only hears the Prs. doctrine when he comes down here and prefers it to the Broad Run Baptist church.

"Monday morning I put my saddle on but the girth broke, and we stopped at Mr. Davis' shop and got a new strap. I picked up my saddle pockets at Dan Wilson's and we were off. Passed Mr. Raymond's place. He was standing at his office door and we rode up to his fence and talked with him. We soon whipped up, went in haste, as Thom said we were in a hurry to reach the Ohio next day.

"Stopped in Salem at Mr. Randolph's tan yard and put dubbin on our shoes to soften the leather. I dipped my boots in the dubbin box—made him mad—tracked the floor. Pointed out an old apple tree over sixty years old and still bearing—likely planted by Johnny Appleseed. Stopped at Mr. Neely's for dinner and found it choice in every respect—good fried chicken, sweet butter and biscuits.

"Thom knew how to make a horse walk, he kept tapping the whip with almost every step and my horse had to sometimes trot to keep up. With this steady gait we reached Martin's before dark. There we met President Sam Huston [*sic*], who was going to Clarksburg on business—he was president of the Republic of Texas. He was a severe-looking man, but was of kindly disposition.

"Next day we pushed the horses right along, keeping them at a good walk. Saw a boy carrying a smaller one on a pillow in front of him on a horse—had been bear hunting, said if we kept our eyes open we might see one. When the sun was over our heads we rested for an hour and disposed of a jolly good snack that Mistress Martin had packed for us and fed our horses sheaf oats that I got from a field nearby, and Thom sent me to the cabin to pay for them. There I found a woman with a baby, but she refused the pay, so I gave her baby a cent with a hole in it to hang around its neck to cut teeth on. Thom seems to have a strong streak of honesty in him to pay for that little bunch of provender to feed our beasts.

"Got to Mistress Glimes hotel in Parkersburg and had some sweet beer and sugar cakes. She keeps the beer in a jug hanging in the well, and it is refreshing. Thom sent some love apples to his aunt.

"Then we went to see Mr. Smith's bank. He showed us some beautiful Spanish molded dollars and American double eagles nearly the same size as the dollar and worth twenty times as much. Then to the Little Kanawha River where we went to swim to wash off the sweat before supper.

"Thursday we were up early to see Mun's father. He is erect and straight as an arrow, he has light hair and sideburn whiskers. On the road back we passed a corn field, and it being early saw several squirrels running along the fence—it was not time to eat or feed, so we didn't stop. At midday we stopped at a farm house where we had a drink of water and bought corn for our horses, for which we paid a levy of 9 pence for twenty-three ears.

We stopped to feed and opened our snack, and my but it was good. A shower came up lasting about half an hour, cooling the air, and my how we slept.

"We had an early morning start again, cool and the horses seemed to know they were going home. Stopped at Neely's and found Miss Mary reading the English Reader, or Elegant Selections in Prose and Poetry by Lindley Murray. This gave me a home feeling, as it was the same reader I was using.

"Met a man very much dressed, a black stock and his coat tails buttoned up behind to prevent soiling. Thom said he always dressed like that when going to meeting at Broad Run.

"Saw a man burying one of his negroes. They carried the coffin from the cabin and buried him in the field. It was a nice black coffin and the grave was deep. Thom said he felt sorry for the race, thought they should have a chance and be taught to read so they could read the Bible."

A Long-Minded Man

Charley Stewart dide jan 9 age 71
1913 ware in war under Lee

"AND that's as far as he will go," people said of the mediocre schoolteacher of whom nothing much was expected in the Civil War and to whom nothing much came at the beginning. Major Thomas Jonathan Jackson still smacked of his native Virginia mountains, despite the regulation uniform he had been wearing for ten years as a Physics professor at the Virginia Military Institute in Lexington. Since VMI was mainly a state-supported school, the Governor ordered the upper-class drill cadets to Richmond to help train raw recruits at Camp Lee. Major Jackson was to escort the boys to the Confederate capital. The order arrived on Sunday morning, April 20, 1861. Jackson set the departure hour for one o'clock that afternoon.

The cadets, wildly excited to get started on a war they knew nothing about, were in marching formation on the VMI parade ground fifteen minutes ahead of time. "Typical, typical," they grumbled among themselves impatiently, "old Jack's waiting to start until the exact time he said he would." He'd had his preacher pray over the boys who were leaving, and old Tom Fool was on the grounds himself, doing nothing, just looking up at the big tower clock.

The appointed hour neared. In the tensing silence a sound was heard. It was the hand of the tower clock wrenching out another minute. Bong! The clock struck one. "Forward, march!" Drumbeats throbbed to every corner of the school grounds, and

Major Jackson marched his cadets out of the parade ground and onto the Virginia Turnpike. Greening hills on either side of the Valley road marked off the far distance.

In Richmond, the cadets were put to work doing their willing bit at the training camp on the Fair Grounds. April went on into a rushing miracle of yesterday's budding elms showing precise young leaves lined up exactly on either side of a thin branch. And Major Jackson, after being lost to and from the world of affairs as an obscure schoolteacher, was put behind a menial desk in the Engineering Department. He had been in such backwash predicaments before and promptly set about getting himself out of this one—by employing the two practiced mottoes he lived by.

The first he had adopted as a wistful teen-ager at West Point, an outsider who had made his entrance into the fashionable school wearing a full suit of homespun. Along with working his heart out to stay in the place, he read a book not on the West Point curriculum, *The Book of Behaviour.* There he found a motto so appealing he wrote it down against forgetting in his school copybook: "You can be whatever you will be." The second and gradually all-encompassing maxim he found in the Bible while he was a young soldier of no particular distinction in Mexico, but consumed with longing to be a man honored in his own right: "All things work together for good to those who love God." This he wrote on his soul.

Both maxims were so familiar as to be trite, but the variable application of them was signally Jackson's own. He had lent God quite a hand in obtaining his VMI professorship when he was twenty-seven, and he used something of the same combination of faith-with-works in Richmond.

He neatly stacked the day's scheduled paperwork at a far side of the desk that was so distasteful to him. Having cleared himself a working space, he penned a letter to the most influential person of his acquaintance at the moment, a former Lexington neighbor, now Governor of Virginia.

In tight, irregular handwriting, but leaving wide margins, he expressed his dissatisfaction with his present position and urged the Governor to do something about it. A courteous letter, but

written in a tone of assured confidence. If given the chance, he
could be of military value to the state.

At his desk in the Capitol Building, Governor Letcher gave
the letter thoughtful consideration. In mulling his erstwhile Lexington neighbor's request, he remembered a Lexington quip: For
a man to be so socially dull, he must have made a study of it.
Major Jackson's eccentricities brightened up many a dinner-table
conversation. One of the stories that so amused the conformist
society of the insular village carried over from the Mexican cam-
paign. Coolly, all but singlehanded and under murderous fire,
Lieutenant Jackson had held his position in the storming of Cha-
pultepec Castle—because, as he explained with disconcerting
honesty afterward, he had not been ordered to retreat.

And then there was the VMI joke about the afternoon Major
Jackson was called into the headmaster's office, who soon was
called out on another matter, asked Jackson to wait, then forgot
all about him and went home. Next morning there was Major
Jackson, sitting bolt upright in an office chair exactly as the Superintendent had left him the afternoon before! Superintendent
Smith was flabbergasted; the cadets, when the incident leaked
out, were hilarious.

As the stories came to the Governor's mind more sharply
edged than when he had heard them told as jokes, they thrust
through the thin surface of entertainment to a deeper potential.
The sacred soil of Virginia was being threatened by invasion by
the Northern foe at its most strategic point, the border town of
Harpers Ferry at the northeast tip of the state. And Honest John
Letcher took a chance.

At the next day's session of the Virginia Convention, he pro-
posed that Major Thomas J. Jackson be commissioned Colonel,
in command of the Volunteer Army at Harpers Ferry. The pro-
posal met with a questioning buzz among the Convention members, most of whom had never heard of Jackson. A spokesman
came to his feet and asked, "Who is this Major Jackson that we
should commit to him so responsible a post?" The answer came
in ringing tones, "He is a man who, if ordered to hold his post,

will never leave it to be occupied by the enemy." The commission was unanimously approved.

When the news filtered into the hinterlands of his rise in rank so soon, people were surprised. "A singlehanded fighter," they granted, but, appalled at his being given the Harpers Ferry command, "not a strategist!"

En route to his new command, Jackson wrote his wife Anna of his promotion. "This is the post I prefer above all others. Little one, do not be concerned about your husband, for our kind Heavenly Father will give every needful benefit."

Exactly ten days after Jackson had marched his cadets up the Valley turnpike bound for Richmond, he brought his youthful company from Richmond to Harpers Ferry—by train.

Harpers Ferry already was a rendezvous for Virginia troops of all sizes and descriptions, with more pouring in daily. A group of loafers on the station platform, waiting for the real diversion of watching the big B. and O. train go thundering by from Washington, cast only slightly interested glances at the newcomers scrambling down the car steps of the little train that came in from the south over a rickety spur line. Their curiosity was more for the boys in their saucy blue school uniforms than for the nondescript man who led them off to the barracks along the railroad tracks.

As the newly commissioned Colonel in command of the Volunteer Army occupying the town, Jackson arrived on the scene virtually unknown.

And what a scene it was! The small army was in wildest confusion; but glamorous confusion. It was like an unrehearsed pageant of war in tumultuous color. There was as yet no evidence of the trim gray uniforms the hastily formed Confederacy would soon start issuing. The fashion of the day, especially among officers of their own independent companies, was the wearing of brilliant sashes, vividly dyed kid gauntlets, and white plumes or jaunty red pompoms on their wide-brimmed hats. It was like war in a gay play in which a troop of cavalry, mounted on their own blooded horses, goes riding through the town singing a rollicking song: "If you want to have a good time, j'ine the cavalry, j'ine the cavalry."

Even the setting was glamorous. The historic town, with its steep streets and red-brick houses clinging to its hillsides, had a romantic charm. In the near distance rose the majestic Blue Ridge, its white dogwood and young green of forest trees cut through by granite grandeur. At the town's edge two rivers met in head-on clash: the sun-sparkling waters of the Shenandoah rippling in through a curving gap in the mountains and the Potomac, whose dark flow marked the dividing line between Virginia and Maryland. United by torrent at Harpers Ferry into one strong river, the Potomac flowed southeast to the sea. Along the river's edge of the town and on over an iron bridge to the Virginia shore ran the railroad tracks. A sense of power was given the scene by the gleaming engines of the B. and O. that whistled and roared over the steel rails. To the boys from the land of stage coaches, those iron horses spitting black smoke and fire sparks was a sight worth seeing!

No less stirring was the row of brick buildings by the railroad tracks: the United States Armory and engine house. The Rifle Works, the arsenal started by George Washington, had made Harpers Ferry an important defense point for a struggling young country.

Only a short year and a half before, the Arsenal still had been important enough for John Brown's attempted seizure of it as part of his plan to incite slaves to armed revolt. The young Virginians were quartered near the little engine house where John Brown had made his last stand. Old John Brown had been hung for treason. The boys who had been marshaled out of the state's military school for the first time under Jackson and who had stood starkly silent honor-guard duty during that awesome hanging in nearby Charlestown thrilled afresh at the remembered solemn pronouncement over his finally dangling body. "So die all enemies of Virginia!"

Northern church bells had tolled for the dead patriarch, Southern anger mounted, and at Harpers Ferry the disturbing time thereafter was spanned by the acrid smell of smoke that

drifted on the high winds of spring from the blackened ruins of
the arsenal.

Just two weeks before, a detachment of Federal soldiers, sta-
tioned here to protect government property, had finished what
John Brown had started. They set fire to the arsenal before they
made an orderly retreat as the larger force of Virginia militia
approached. The blackened ruins of the arsenal, the freshly
green woods of the Blue Ridge—it was a magnificent setting for
the opening of the most tragic drama America had ever known.

And the only undramatic figure in it was the man who was to
stage the opening scene.

He rode no prancing steed. Despite the incongruity of an enormous pair of worn cavalry boots that reached to his knees, he
rode no horse at all when he took over his new command. There
was no gold braid or lace on the plain coat of his old VMI uniform. His hat was a fading blue forage cap he wore pulled so far
over his forehead he had to raise his bearded chin to see out,
although apparently he walked unseeing through the milling
town. Often during the initial days of his command his fast walk
brought him to an abstracted halt on the river bank near the
barracks, where he stood slackly, lost in distances of his own.

An army correspondent for a Southern newspaper could not
resist including a sketch of the Commander, in his Harpers
Ferry report. "The queer apparition of the ex-Professor on the
field excited great merriment. The Old Dominion must be woe-
fully deficient in military men if this was the best she could do.
The new Colonel is not at all like a commanding officer. His
manner is awkward, he has little to say to anybody, and there is
a painful want in him of all the 'pride, pomp and circumstance of
glorious warfare.' "

The correspondent's impression was so generally shared in
Harpers Ferry that the embarrassed cadets averted their eyes
from the covert smiles of amused observers. Rank and file, his
raw army tended to dismiss this absent-minded Colonel Jackson,
with the big hands and feet of a farmer, as one officer who
wouldn't bother them much. His sole insignia of rank was the
sheathed saber he had carried in Mexico and now carried again

at his belt. It was sizable, and the way it banged heavily against his rapid stride made even that distinction ludicrous. Except for a scattering of minor skirmishes throughout the country, there wasn't any war yet, nothing that called for swordplay. And in Harpers Ferry it was only the pageantry of war.

The day was still to come when Jackson, his hand raised to heaven and passion unleashed, would swoop furiously down on the unsuspecting enemy with the swift terribleness of lightning. But meanwhile he did have an opportunity for trying out his theory that in war—as in many things else—mystery is the key to success.

He was called upon in his quarters by a committee from the Maryland State Legislature. He was unusually courteous in his stiffly formal greeting, for it was the ardent hope of the Confederacy that wavering Maryland would join the Southern cause. But to the politicians' suave quizzing as to the Colonel's plans for defending Harpers Ferry, Jackson listened attentively—in silence.

One of the legislators, sitting apart near the desk cleared of everything except Jackson's Bible and stationery kit, and in speculative view of the sheathed sword standing handily in a corner by the door, took no part in the abortive questioning. Rather, he studied this Bible-reading, sword-carrying Colonel, trying to figure some means to responsive approach.

The chiseled face, with the impassive blue gaze and the determined line of mouth only slightly softened by a wavy brown beard, was like rock against weather.

With that observation, the legislator threw diplomacy to the winds and asked a blunt question. "Colonel, how many troops do you have?"

To this question Jackson had a ready answer. He even smiled —a charming smile—"I would like to have Lincoln think I have ten thousand."

The disgruntled politicians left to take the train back to Baltimore, knowing the way of his mind no more than when they had come.

Nor did he confide his plans to his wife, Anna. He described his Harpers Ferry quarters to her—an upstairs room in an "elegant mansion." "I have a nice green yard and if only you were here how much we could enjoy it together." This was followed by a note in teasing vein. "You say your husband doesn't write you any news. I suppose you mean military news, for I have written you a great deal about how much your *esposo* loves you. What do you want with military news?"

Of a truth, there was no great military news to tell. Jackson's troops numbered a pittance of the sum he would like to have had Lincoln think, and the ammunition supply was entirely inadequate for active defense of Harpers Ferry. Toward that inevitability, during the tightening days of early May, he started bringing order out of chaos. His experience in organizing an army was slight, but he had set his Lexington house in order in the only way he knew. That impossible, incredible, pedantic man Jackson, people said, running *his* house like clockwork, military clockwork—the moment the beat of the VMI drum was heard, summoning the boys into marching line for the mess hall, any and everyone in Jackson's house filed into the dining room. Absurd!

People would have been surprised to know that the paradoxical Jackson gave a personal touch to that systematic order—love of a place and the richness of life in it, telling Anna joyously of this house, the only home of his own he'd ever had, "every door on a golden hinge swinging softly."

Having organized his personal life and his own home in which so briefly he had been so happy, now, on a vastly wider scale, he set about organizing his army; prosaically, according to the work at hand.

Dashing Jeb Stuart, who wore a peacock feather in his hat, was assigned the cavalry command. With the *élan* of a true cavalier, Stuart, with his plumed and sashed company mounted on horses as fine as their pistols, patrolled the long riverfront to report its terrain and signs of enemy activity.

Gallant Turner Ashby, who had led the vanguard of Virginia militia into Harpers Ferry on a splendid white horse, was put in command of the artillery. The immediate call on Ashby's courage was to convert his company into an engineering outfit for the grubby duty of salvaging any machinery not too badly damaged by the arsenal fire for the manufacture of arms, and convert it to Confederate use.

Sandy Pendleton, the son of a Lexington friend and a West Point graduate, there with a company of students from a divinity college, was made battery commander. The battery consisted of whatever long-range arms were left in the Rifle Works, a few light field pieces without caissons to carry them or horses to haul them, and insufficient harness. Pendleton's company of fellow students got in a little persuasive practice on neighborhood farmers and reaped a harvest of several strong horse carts. From the wheels and axles the young divines contrived some sturdy caissons, and from farm gear and rope rigged up harness for pulling the field guns by hand.

Down by the railroad tracks the cadets again were put to work drilling raw recruits, who now were streaming in by the ill-assorted hordes from all over the South. There was a smattering of privately uniformed companies, each flagrantly different, but whether uniformed, in debonair straw hat or rakish coonskin cap, there was a dismaying alikeness to these eager volunteers. They all came equipped, bearing every sort of weapon known to more or less peaceful man: muskets grown rusty in state armories, squirrel rifles, pistols, and a goodly portion of ancient guns taken down from log walls. Said one of these long hunters from the hills with laconic pride in his trusty flintlock, "Hit's not much for purty, but hits hell for stout." And their enthusiastic confidence that before summer was over they could lick some dim remote foe named the Yankee was equaled only by their complete lack of military training.

The dismayed cadets were as keen as anybody about getting this war started and over with, but nothing in the Richmond encampment had prepared them for the monumental task of trying to make soldiers out of the awkward squads they faced. Worse, here they would be directly under Old Jack's coldly critical eye. Then, gradually, they made a not altogether welcome discovery. They might have been paralyzed with boredom by Old Jack's

unimaginative lectures at school and incensed at his being so unfair, so hateful as to give even his best students a poor mark if
they so much as forgot to initial a perfectly worked-out tactical
problem; but somewhat to their surprise they were finding they
had learned something in that stuffy schoolroom after all. It was
ironical—the irony when you laugh through gritted teeth. Here
they were, being just as unreasonable, just as insistent on perfec-
tion with the awkward squads. The men thought their young
drillmasters unnecessarily fussy about presenting arms and "all
that geeing and hawing, wheeling about and walking just so," as
a farmer termed the marching and countermarching, a lot of
foolishness.

It was grueling work, drill, drill, all morning and all afternoon. There was no glamour to it but the boys kept at it. Fires
began to flicker and glow through the black night heights—
thinly scattered, but representing a growing fortification around
the town. By now the deepening green of forest was broken by
the gay flame of wild azalea and the pent-up crimson of rhododendron.

Jackson himself didn't seem to do much. He held staff meetings, occasionally leaning slightly forward in his chair to listen
more closely and nod approvingly. "Good, good." And he con-
fided nothing. He went to church on Sunday and dozed through
the sermon, and periodically inspected the progress of the artillery division. The battery boasted four guns put into workable
condition, although Pendleton hadn't wasted precious cannon
balls to prove it. But there would come a day when the young
Virginians would so like the gospel preached by those four can-
nons that they'd affectionately call the big makeshift guns Mat-
thew, Mark, Luke, and John.

Meanwhile, stern of countenance, the Colonel reviewed his infantry troops. He still wore no gold or tinsel, although now he
rode a horse, which was, as one of his aghast men described in a
letter, "the damndest-looking horse God ever put legs under."
His men would have been astonished to know that Jackson actually had paid the Confederacy for the fat, short-legged sorrel that
seemed to have about as much life as a wad of old hair combings.

And they'd have been incredulous had they known Jackson had
bought the horse as an eventual present to his wife; had, moreover, described its gait to her as being as "comfortable as a rock-
ing chair."

By another spring, his men would cheerfully follow the man
in the shabby coat astride a sorrel nag "across hell on a rotten
log." And they'd joke about Little Sorrel. "That horse don't know
but one way to run," they'd say, "and that's toward the enemy."

Yet even in May of 1861, the awkward squads, not so awkward now, were saluting the Colonel respectfully. Something of
Jackson's iron nerve was being instilled into his army. Less frequently these days did he go on from his review and come to a
preoccupied halt by the river bank, his blue-eyed glint under the
visor of his cap beyond reach of the casual observer. When that
did occur, there were no covert smiles. Rank and file, his forming
army was undergoing a tentative change of judgment about its
commander, soberly expressed by a foot soldier in homespun.
"He looks like a long-minded man."

In his quarters, Jackson continued to write love letters to his
wife, wishing she were here with him to enjoy the beautiful
flowers in the yard and gardens of the town: "But your sweet,
sunny little face is what I long most of all to see. Little one, you
are so precious to somebody's heart."

By mid-May the theater for the tremendous drama of the
American Civil War was almost arranged. And the Baltimore
and Ohio Railroad ran squarely across the stage. From its eastern
approach to Harpers Ferry through a narrow mountain pass on
the Maryland shore of the Potomac, over the bridge into Virginia, the B. and O. ran double tracked to the railroad center at
Martinsburg, thirty miles away. Ever since Jackson's arrival he
had noted with sharpening shrewdness the enormous freight
traffic the line carried. Eastbound freight cars were piled high
with coal from western Maryland and Virginia. The Federal authorities were accumulating coal on the eastern seaboard. Night
and day the heavily loaded coal cars pounded their way through
town, bound for Baltimore and Washington. Night and day they
rattled back, filled with equipment for the Union forces gather-

ing strength in central and western Virginia. Coming or going, the engines gave forth with a peculiar, shrieking whistle.

And one evening in his quarters, when the night world in the yard outside knew how to keep its secrets too—the bright purity of moonlight important to the dimness of the night's dark—he drew a fresh sheet of paper from the neat stack on his desk and penned a businesslike note to the president of the Baltimore and Ohio Railroad.

"The noise of your trains is intolerable. My men find their repose disturbed by them each night. You will have to work out some other method of operating them."

In his elaborate Baltimore office the president, Mr. John Garret, read the note with rage. He was having enough trouble keeping his railroad in operation as it was, without some upstart Colonel in Harpers Ferry telling him how to run his business.

Already he'd had to reschedule passenger trains because of reported April panic along the line—harassed conductors assuring menacing crowds at stops flying the Confederate flag that absolutely nobody except Southern sympathizers were on the train; at stations flying the Stars and Stripes conductors swearing that only those loyal to the Union rode the cars. And climbing into the middle mountain country, nervous engineers sent the train through whistle stops of divided sentiment like a dose of salts. With Baltimore and Washington in imminent danger of being cut off by railroad, mail and passenger service had been diverted around hazardous points by river or canal.

Thus far the B. and O. president had kept the profitable freight traffic open, transporting Union supplies, largely through the influence of Major General McClellan in Washington. Now here he was, being pressured by the Confederate commander at Harpers Ferry.

John Garret was a dominant man, endowed with a gift for leadership; upon occasion he could be a diplomat. On narrow-eyed second reading of Jackson's note, he recognized something of those same qualities. He strongly doubted that hocus-pocus about his trains keeping the rumored thousands of healthy men awake nights. Enraged though Garret was, this was one of those

occasions that called for diplomacy. On so slender a thread hung
the fate of his entire main line. The railroad president was in no
position to defy the Colonel of the Volunteer Army, a growing
force of untried strength. So, in his reluctantly written reply, he
agreed to work out a system whereby all B. and O. freight trains
would go through Harpers Ferry during the day. And he did.

That done, Jackson wrote a follow-up letter narrowing the
timing of his request, to the effect that the ear-splitting whistles
of the engines disrupted the routine morning and afternoon drill
practice. Mr. Garret must have all trains, eastbound and westbound, scheduled to go through between the noonday hours of
eleven and one.

More grudgingly, the helpless Mr. Garret complied. There
was no holding closed the Harpers Ferry curtain now.

It opened on a scene showing the white blackberry bloom
being blown by the midday breeze into high weeds growing beside the railroad tracks. Crouched in the weeds or waiting
around a bend, hiding behind stone bridge supports or out of
sight on rocky ledges, all along that stretch of double track clear
to Martinsburg, waiting in ambush, was a company of Stuart's
cavalry, Ashby's artillery, Pendleton's ministerial cannoneers;
and from the infantry, boys with hearts pounding deafeningly
gripped guns, at last tensed for action. It wasn't exactly the sort
of action they'd expect from prudish Old Jack, but it was exciting.

At noon, engine whistles shrieking, rails rattling and rum-
bling under their loads, eastbound and westbound, the trains all
came through and Jackson's men captured them, every one.

Soon thereafter, the people living along the Virginia turnpike
began being treated to an amazing sight, stemming from an
order received by Jackson. The more cautious head of the whole
Confederate army, Major General Johnson, ordered Jackson to
burn *all* the seized railroad property at Martinsburg. Like the
dutiful soldier he was, Jackson obeyed. Thoroughly the torch
was set to almost fifty locomotives; for miles along the B. and O.
tracks, warped coal cars burned red hot.

In a skirmish incidental to the burning of the captured Martinsburg cars, Jeb Stuart had picked up some Federal stationery and impishly presented a piece to Jackson. It was patriotically embellished with picture of a statue of Liberty and the caption, in red, white, and blue, "On to Victory!" Jackson used it to write Anna something of the skirmish, telling her that his brigade, officers and men, had behaved beautifully but were anxious for a real battle. And it was with genuine sadness that he went on to tell his darling about the railroad destruction he had wrought.

"If the cost of the property could have been spent disseminating the gospel of the Prince of Peace, how much good might have been expended."

Then, out of his Harpers Ferry plan, made in secret and so daringly executed, came another, even greater, idea. The supplies from the Harpers Ferry coup had been a rich prize for his needful army, and he had helped himself to four small locomotives, not too heavy to go over the rickety spur line to Winchester and eventually to Richmond. Now, having followed his Martinsburg order, he took another survey of the locomotives. They were badly scorched and blistered by the heat, but comparatively little of the iron engines had been destroyed. Still, his bulky booty presented problems. The best of the locomotives were too big to go over the poorly built Winchester line but, challenged lift of head and heart, there was another way!

And that was when the people along the Valley turnpike began seeing the astounding sight of railroad locomotives being hauled down the dusty road by mule team, four abreast and ten mules deep, filling the pike from side to side, with the huge iron horses being dragged along by ropes, creaking protest and careening drunkenly on the curves. Muscled men added their strength, their swearing and wild singing to the racket, and often shots in answer to the crackle of musketry from Yankee snipers, as the startling procession went onward to its triumphantly shouted destination, "On to Strasburg!"

Martinsburg, Bunker Hill, Charlestown, Winchester, and on to Strasburg where the engines were again put on rails. These were Southern rails that could connect with the entire Confederate railroad system. The connection was made where the tracks ran beside a stream called Bull Run, at a little junction called Manassas.

Jackson's beloved South needed engine power.

Not a single great battle had yet been fought. Nevertheless, as the pageant in iron wound on down the Valley road from spring into summer, curiosity about the still little-known man who staged it mounted like slow delight.

"Who is this General Jackson," people said, "who prays to God and steals B. and O. locomotives?"

. . . And then it would be spring again, and on an early May Sunday in 1863 the immortal Stonewall would come to his ending, at the height of his most dramatic daring. In the moonlit shadows of The Wilderness, riding with his battle hand aloft, there would be a flash of guns and he would be shot, mistakenly, by his own men. He would not die of his wounds, but from pneumonia contracted after his historic cracker-barrel conference in the woods by lantern light with his friend Robert E. Lee. That night, with the dew lying like frost on the ground, he would sleep in the woods, and waken to notice his aide without covering. Gently the General would cover the sleeping young soldier with his own ragged coat.

Reprisal

Les Blake age 72 dide augus 18 1913
war solder and robbed folks

AS the Civil War accelerated, a great deal of Appalachian military action on both sides took the form of raids and counterraids. The Confederate Generals William Jones and John Imboden are the best known of the Virginians, and General Jones the most hated by his victims. West Virginia's McNeill Rangers were organized by the head of the McNeill family, whose pre-Revolutionary land grant covered hundreds of acres of rich bottom land and mountain timber in the South Branch country. Very quickly the boldness of the Rebel rangers attracted congenial volunteers from Maryland. General Phil Sheridan, himself a raider of repute, acclaimed the McNeill Rangers the most dangerous of all the bushwhackers. In western North Carolina and eastern Tennessee, Colonel George Kirk and his mounted regiment of irregular Federal soldiers are remembered as Kirk's marauding robber band.

Despite being encumbered by the horses, cattle, and even prisoners they carried off, all the dreaded raiders rode far and wide. Meanwhile the skirmishes over timbered knolls and farmers' fields that had marked the devastating beginning of the highland War Amongst Us persisted between foot soldiers of both armies, impeded only by short rations.

When I was teaching school in the North Carolina mountains, I heard about a retaliatory episode of the war's second summer, which occurred in Kirk's locality and involved the ruse of the wild turkey's rasping cry.

Since Indian days the virtuosity of hunters has been challenged by that most desirable and wariest of game birds, the strictly American wild turkey. Experienced woodsmen have long played upon their familiarity with the arrogant bird's habits. They know that turkeys roost in folded-wing flocks at night in trees; that they travel in strutting flocks to their early-morning feeding ground; that, if frightened while scratching for mast, they scatter, but will keep in communication during the day by repeated calls to one another. The skilled hunter hides in the woods, imitates the turkey's raucous cry, and calls in the singles.

In the storied episode of the war-hungered Blue Ridge, the wild turkey afforded a very plausible excuse for a gunner to lurk in a woods unsuspected of avenging purpose.

. . . For the full time of year, things were looking lean. The cornfield was nothing but a slantwise piece of ground torn up by its roots, with here and there a corn stalk lying dried and tramped on by soldier shoes. The open log barn cried alike for plundered horse and hay, and the woods standing close by seemed not so friendly now that the cow bells were silent in it. The unpainted slab house looked starved; perhaps a few hens, scratching more from habit than hope in the barren yard, made it seem so. A lone pig rooted near the doorstep.

"Hit's got to live till butcherin' time," said the woman of the house, looking out at it. "Hit's our meat for the rest of the winter."

"Don't you go to be troubled, Clarinda. This war'll be over by winter, then I'll be home to stay and fill that old smokehouse full to bustin' with wild meat—and hit's better'n hog meat any day."

"Oh, Davy!" The woman, who was not very old—seventeen and looking not a day over—turned from the sorry outdoors to her husband and was heartened. He was in Lee's gray, to be sure, but he was here; hers for a day and night anyway. "Oh, Davy, hit's so good to have you. I wish you never would go back to that old army."

"Ssh—what a thing to say! They *need* me down yonder."

She had a quick and unworthy thought, this girl-wife did, that she and the babe needed him too. And with the thought came back that sucked-dry feeling around her heart that had been so much there since Davy had gone off warring. But she hid her fears under a little prayer and said, "Shore, that's what I know. We'll kill us a chicken and have dumplin's you can think about till you git home ag'in."

"Dumplin's?"

She nodded triumphantly. "I got a smidgen of flour hid away under the bed tick."

And they were very gay while she wrung a fowl's neck and plucked its feathers off. David plagued and deviled her and took on generally till she declared they wouldn't be worth shucks, neither chicken nor dumplings! Contentedly the while, Matt, the baby, pushed a low stool back and forth across the floor. Once, after sober consideration, he backed up to it and sat down—smack—missing the stool entirely, his legs spread wide, his eyes wide too. How they laughed! With Davy catching the surprised little fellow up in his arms and hugging him.

An hour later found him still holding the child, jiggling it up and down on his knee, with the sun full on them both. And Davy knew to his bones the content of an August noon in the mountains, clear and hot and good to feel.

"Now," said Clarinda. The chicken he had been smelling for an hour was piled brown and brave on a platter, and the dumplings were floating in the best bowl.

Over the baby's rumpled towhead their eyes met in full appreciation of the feast; the riotous gaiety that goes with deliberate improvidence, the full consciousness of a security that cannot last, and the sudden sucked-dry feeling in both their breasts. The baby wriggled down from his father's loosened hold and made a gleeful lurch toward the table. But before ever he reached it, before either of them could dart to haul him back, a sound broke up the whole plan of the feast. The dull, even sound of men marching down a dirt road.

Clarinda stood paralyzed, remembering whispered outrages in other neighborhoods at the hands of Kirk's marauders. David

slid to a shadow by the door where he could look down the road
and see dust rising about as high as the berry bushes alongside,
and men in blue above it. Just a hantel of them—raggedy and
bobtail, for the war had been going on two years now. They
might be furriners or they might be neighbors, but whichever
they were, they were Federals.

With a step backward, keeping his eye all the while on the
road coming toward the house, he felt for the laurel hooks on the
wall where his gun rested.

"Davy!" It was protest against all violence; it was fear; it was
indignation at this interruption of their time together. "Hide in
the loft!" At the same time, with presence of mind, Clarinda
grabbed up a chicken that was just stepping over the threshold.
It squawked in fright as she flung up the lid of a chest by the
fireplace and dropped it in. "That's one chicken they won't git,"
grimly. She gave up as lost another that had evaded her clutch
and now was flying and running in front of the advancing terror,
its wings flapping. Then, imploringly, "Davy!" as he continued
to stand ill-concealed in the door shadow.

By now, the first of the straggling file of blue was even with
the farthest corner of the yard. For an instant David experienced
the same sensation he might have had in a smoke-filled woods
while he waited behind a tree for some instinct of war to guide
him in his next move. But the deadly casualness did not last the
instant out. For the baby, catching sight of the strange men,
flung both his arms about his father's legs and clung to him for
dear life. David looked down. He saw the little lad venture to
show his face for another peek at the moving, looming awfulness
out front, then wiggle back to safety. David felt him, close and
depending. He dropped his hand to the flaxen head. A second
chicken with beady scared eyes and red comb was being dropped
by Clarinda's resolute hand into the chest.

"Take away my plate, and you and the youngin eat." He
swung up the ladder into the loft.

Even though the soldiers could turn in anywhere now—for
the fence out front was broken and scattered—she took time to
go with him, with her eyes, into his hiding. Then, her young

mouth old, she hurried the platter of chicken and all but a small dish of dumplings into the cupboard. Mechanically she sat shoveling dough into the youngin's mouth while he lolled against her, pushing the table edge luxuriously with bare toes. His gaze upon her was contented; the strange men were forgotten.

Up in the loft David lay on the floor, propped up on one elbow, peering out through a crack in the logs. He did not recognize any of the intruders, so calculated they were furriners. Beside him was his gun, ready to pick up and aim down the loft hole if they showed any meanness when they came in.

But he heard an order cracked out. The marching column double-quicked on past the house, with the pig ambling out to see why and the midday sun hurrying to hit the muzzles of briskened arms. David was surprised. Evidently this was not just a foraging party—perhaps these men had been cut off from their company. Nevertheless, they appeared, through the dust they were raising, ready to drop, and hungry. Not nearly so hungry as all of Lee's men looked, however.

Had this observation occurred to him at any other time except now—under fire, in camp, retreating, advancing—it would have stuck in his gizzard. But the feel of his least one was still warm with him, and the last hour with his wife-woman had made fighting for some faraway and absent cause not worth more than a slight rise of emotion that dropped again quickly. Abstractedly, he followed the enemy by with no especial ill-will.

Until one, with his blue coat open and his whitish shirt showing, reached out and with a deft swiping of hand and foot pulled the pig into the middle of the column. There was the sound of muffled laughter and pig squeals. The rear guard marched close and irregularly down the road, with the meat that was to have lasted Davy's homefolks all winter marching with it.

Through the crack, the glint of sun on Federal muzzles made a blazing smear in front of the watcher's eyes.

From below came a quick scraping of chair and cautious, "Davy, they're gone. But better you stay up thar a piece—I'll keep the chicken hotted."

There was no answer. A moment earlier David had risen, on

high toes had stepped across to the low window hole, and dropped with his gun to the ground.

Stealing from house to barn to cedar to fence corner, he made the woods in safety. Keeping in their shelter, he skirted the upper side of the looted cornfield, then dropped abruptly with it and the road and the blue men marching to a cloistered level spot. Looking back, he could no longer see the chimney of his house, although he was not many yards away.

Here the company halted. Immediately the word was given, there was a willing scramble for firewood and a good deal of scuffling over who would stick the hog. One big soldier good-humoredly pawed the others off, grabbed the squealing animal, and straddled it; another, with his sleeves up and his knife out, deftly jabbed into the middle of a grunt.

Taking quick stock of the trees about him, David chose a tall sycamore with a magnificent spread. He was up it in a minute. Now he could see his chimney smoke, his whole house and yard sitting bare in the sun. Looking the other way, he could see the barbecue blaze shimmering in the noonday heat. The man with his sleeves rolled up now had his right arm up to the elbow inside the male brute's belly-slit. From his place of vantage David looked on. That was a job of work for Clarinda this winter when he was far away and the weather bitter and food for the youngin scarce. She would not pull and yank like that, but stick her brown arm in and work and loosen carefully. He did not reflect further; a single word was in his mind. War. Without any excitation of feeling, he gave a wild-turkey call.

Two of the men lying on their backs at a distance from the butchering scene raised their heads and listened. After a time, David repeated it. A third soldier on yon side the fire wheeled around. "Turkey! Boys, it's a feast!" He picked up his gun and made for the woods, with laughter and advice thrown after him.

Up in the sycamore the Confederate smiled and with his own weapon leveled, watched the eagerness, yet prudence, of the other's approach. To guide him came again the wild-game cry. It was not a big woods, nor uncommon deep, and so, sun-speckled.

From sun to shadow the man in blue came on, and when he got near enough for David to see that he was a pleasant enough fellow with food in his beard, he fired. The Yankee dropped with a bullet hole in his chest and his gun teetering across his body. He lay groaning. David turned his face homeward. There in the yard was Clarinda looking for him distractedly. Again sounded the grating turkey call, this time as if from a greater distance.

The two men flat on their backs down in the camp raised up as before and one of them got on his feet.

"Old Joe must have missed. Guess I'll have to go bring down that gobbler myself."

The pig was now swung up on an improvised spit over the fire, and there was even more joshing this hunter than there had been the first. The Federal army's heart was growing bigger as its nostrils filled with wood smoke and the first smoking of hog juice on the flame.

When the second man, turkey hunting and looking up, came into David's particular patch of sun, he almost stumbled over the writhing body of his comrade. But before he could cry out or take aim or even wholly regain his balance, the second shot rang out. He swayed and toppled, and fell against the tree in a half-sitting posture, quite dead. It struck David as an odd sight to be in a bright patch of sun. A chicken came wandering in to share it with him. It seemed unsteady on its legs, a little dazed. He recognized it as the one that had fled wildly down the road. Forlorn thing. With kindly, absorbing pleasure David watched it snatch up in its beak an insect from out of the earth. Then, as if his cue had been given, he started, and gave at once the warning scatter call of the grouse.

Down around the fire a man with his coat open and white shirt showing looked up sharply; dropped his armload of fresh wood abruptly. He said something in a low tone to the man nearest him and five of them followed as he entered cautiously into the woods. David knew by this that they guessed it was no ordinary game bird calling from the thicket. And he experienced a confused and peculiar joy. When the white-shirted leader—the one who had marched away with the pig—came within hearing, David gave the all-clear signal, a low "puk-puk" of the ruffed grouse that preludes its flight.

Evidently the other was as acquainted with the ways of the woods as he, for the Yankee stopped and listened, as if for the rustle of wings that should follow; when none came, he proceeded even more guardedly. He was within range now but David did not fire. His hesitation was due more to an inbred code of respect than to any present studying over the matter— the fellow was no addlepate and he deserved a chance.

David waited. He could see now that the white-shirted one still had down on his cheeks and zest in him for everything. Suddenly he raised his head and their eyes met. For a second there was the shock of actual contact. Then, the vibration still in his arms, his legs, his chest, David presented his musket. But the lock hung up and would not fire. He jerked and yanked. The whole world was a confusion of blue cloth and shining metal. There was no moisture in David's mouth and he could not swallow. He heard distinctly the preliminary click of the Federal trigger. There flashed in his mind all the things a man about to die should think of, but there was no time.

The splintering, crackling sounds were the sycamore branches breaking as he fell down through them, and the sound of the impact of the body on the earth was a peculiar mingling of something dead and something deeply living.

The boy in blue stood with his carbine loosely hanging from his right hand, his mouth open, the oppression so great within him he could not breathe properly.

"See," he pointed tragically as the others came up, "see what I've done!"

In amazement and derision, four of them heard him. But the fifth, an older man who had lived longer and knew more, was silent. He kicked the chicken away from the new puddle of entrails.

Bought Wit Is Best

*John Wise & Newton Wise and Thomas
Wise went to Getsburg for big reyouon
1913*

THE Wise brothers went through the three days of
Gettysburg fighting and were at Appomattox Courthouse when
Lee surrendered. After they came home, the oldest brother,
Uncle John, took it upon himself to be a traveling schoolteacher.
All the education he had to offer he had learned from his great-
grandmother, a woman of culture and refinement who came from
England. Granny Sary had the distinction of having been mar-
ried in a white silk dress and buried in it, and furthermore, she
could read Latin.

Uncle John would ride into a community at the beginning of
winter, after the crops were laid by, and hold school in somebody's house or the church, if there was one. He taught Latin by
rote, long passages from the *Iliad*, and used the Bible as a text-
book reader. One of his quick-minded students once won a prize
at an evening entertainment for his exhibition of the highlanders'
remarkable gift of memory.

The lad recited the twenty-fifth chapter of Genesis, beginning
with the generations of Abraham by a wife of his old age,
naming sons of sons straight through the familiar realism of
Isaac's wife Rebekah, whose children "struggled together within
her. . . . And the Lord said unto her . . . Two manner of
people shall be separated from thy bowels. . . . And when her
days to be delivered were fulfilled, behold, there were twins in

her womb. And the first came out red . . . and they called his name Esau. And after that came his brother out, and his hand took hold on Esau's heel; and his name was called Jacob. . . . And the boys grew. . . . And Isaac loved Esau because he did eat of his venison; but Rebekah loved Jacob. And Jacob sod pottage: and Esau came in from the field, and he was faint." And he sold his birthright to Jacob for a pottage of lentils—and no words wasted. The performance had a fascinated audience. As an attentive parent pondered later, "Hit was about like common."

Uncle John also taught arithmetic and spelling. His graphic methods along the latter line are still vividly remembered. In fact, it was a little girl on the tiptoe edge of grace who told me how to spell tobacco, as she had learned it from her mother. "TOBACCO," she rattled:

> "Three fourth of a cross, a circle complete,
> Upright standing where two semicircles do meet,
> A right angle triangle standing on feet,
> Two semicircles and a circle complete. TOBACCO!"

> "BUZZARD," she added delightedly at my blinking.
> "Bee-U-izzard-izzard-A-R-D!"

John Wise did more than quaintly spark a revival of the learning his people had brought into the mountains. The native teacher affirmed the trait of independence no more important to the survival of highland culture than breathing. This I learned in the course of a walk when the June morning was in the quietness of a thousand hushed noises. I stopped by for a few minutes with an elderly couple taking their ease on the porch of their creekside house. The texture of their remembrance of Uncle John was as sunny and fresh as the morning itself.

"He was a purty man," recalled the woman as she sat finishing a leisurely task she'd brought outdoors. She snapped the last green bean from her lapful and dropped it into the pan beside her. "He stood so tall he touched the rafters, and he talked so proper."

"He wrote a powerful good hand, and taught it too," said her husband, leaning against the open-door frame. He took his pipe from his mouth and let its smoke mingle with the woodsy fragrance of the pine logs stacked against the house wall. "Why, I can shape letters with my toes layin' flat better'n most folks with a goose-quill pen."

His wife, standing up to brush off her dress, slid him a quick sidelong look. "Now, Congress!"

"I was only huntin' for the words to say," he protested, both of them saying admiringly well that their childhood teacher was a man you weren't liable to forget. Congress was just a chunk of a boy when he went to a school Uncle John taught in the new Big Meadows Free Will Baptist Church, and even then had been allowed to attend only after dark when the chores were done, or on snow-blanketed days. His father hadn't needed book learning to plow a straight furrow and saw no sense in it for his oldest son who would heir the property—at first that is.

I gathered that Father changed his mind.

"Deed and truly he did." The oldest son drew comfortably on his pipe. "He was so tickled to have me read some old family deeds for him so he could get the lay of his land straight in his mind, hit's a mercy in this world that there's a locust tree standin' on the place, the way he had me shinnyin' around the ridge cuttin' out the best saplings for Uncle John's fence posts to pay for my schoolin'. A locust post," he explained, "will last a man a hundred years." His explanation conveyed a quality akin to the enduring hardness of locust.

I wondered if Uncle John had charged everyone who went to his school.

"Why Lord, yes." The highlander straightened, and his wife's hand stopped midway in a downward stroke. They were surprised that I asked, it was so ingenerate a thing the teacher had done.

Being a self-respecting man, John Wise naturally respected that trait in others. He did not offer a give-away program. The tuition fee might be paid in money, farm products, or labor. Fathers with a handiwork knack might repair his roof or mend his chimney; a mother present him with her choicest quilt, in appreciation. Usually the youngsters helped defray the cost by doing odd jobs for the teacher, chopping firewood for his church-house schools or caring for his horse. The cost was nominal—a dollar a month. But never in all his dedicated years of traveling the winter mountains did Uncle John Wise give the education he had to offer entirely free. Always, in whatever form, it was paid for.

Here and there through the generations an outstanding figure has risen up out of the irregular grandeur of the southern highlands. In the Kentucky wilderness Daniel Boone unfurled a flag to a new nation, Transylvania, before the American Revolution. George Rogers Clark, with his expeditionary force of Virginia and Kentucky frontiersmen, tall riflemen in homespun and deerhide, boldly set forth on their conquest of the far west. Tennessee's Andrew Jackson, without fear, with sublime faith in his own judgment, was twice elected President. Another outspoken frontiersman, David Crockett, along with Samuel Houston of Pennsylvania, colonized Texas. It was the Presidential decision of a South Carolina backwoodsman, James Polk, to invade Mexico, whereby the boundaries of the nation were widened to include the state of Texas. Out of the Kentucky hills came the Great Emancipator, Abraham Lincoln, hurled to immortality by the same war that brought to light the military genius of western Virginia's Stonewall Jackson. And there were returning soldiers like John Wise, dedicated to helping their people realize their potential through knowledge.

Also, as in every other quarter of the earth, the mountains have their characters and sophisticated highlanders delight in telling anecdotes about them. Such a character was Albert Gallahue, born on a farm in Pine Grove, West Virginia, in 1865, and dubbed The Tall Wahoo from Wetzel County.

Old Gall, as he was called by his familiars, was a veritable bag of bones, and a hank of long hair that suggested he had slept on it several different ways during a restless night. From the time he was a young man and onward, he affected a broad-brimmed black hat, black string ties, and white shirts with brown streaks down their front—Old Gall couldn't spit very good. Nobody has ever claimed that cleanliness was next to godliness in Old Gall's books. But if he gave the rangy impression of being put together loosely in an abstracted moment, he had a mind like a bear trap.

When not working his farm or fox hunting, he indulged his legal bent. Although he was never admitted to the bar, his persuasive eloquence frequently was called into play as trial lawyer in the local courts of justice. Should his client offer the challenge of being guilty as the Devil in the henhouse, Old Gall drew a packed hearing. Unofficially, he held forth on the courthouse steps, telling stories woven out of everything he had ever read, heard, or done.

Fortunately for people who wistfully wish now they had written down some of the fantasia Gall spun on those stone steps, the moment caught, a recent issue of the *West Virginia Hillbilly* carried a sample of the Tall Wahoo's extemporaneous oratory. The founder-editor of the weekly newspaper, Jim Comstock, has a brand of genius himself. He uses his satirical wit as an editorial rapier for upholding the honor of his native Mountain State. Moreover, Jim encourages copious reader material. In this instance, obviously the forewarned contributor was on the spot with expectant pen in hand, for the stinging sample is lengthy.

In brief, the speech was brought on when Young Gall presented so comic a rainy-night appearance at the opera house in Fairmont, where he was a newly entered student in the town's normal school, that he was greeted by a crowd of college jokesters with cat calls. "Where did that yokel come from?" Nothing loath, Gall, finding he had been slyly maneuvered to the front row of seats where there was no place for him, told them. Facing his audience, he removed his dripping black hat and, with a sweeping bow, made a hush-provoking start.

"Ladies and gentlemen, Fellow citizens and Fools. I thank you for your vociferous applause and your most cordial reception, which to me is as unsuspecting as it is flattering.

"If you ask where I hail from, my reply shall be, I hail not from Appomattox and its famous apple tree where the conquering hero wrested the sword of victory from the vanquished foe.

. . . I hail not from lands across the seas, hallowed by painter's brush and poet's song, where gallant knights rode forth with waving plumes and flashing crest. . . . I hail not from the land of palms and southern pines where the balmy jasmine-scented zephyrs wake to ecstasy the living lyre. . . . Nor yet from the vine-covered hills of France. . . . Nor the storied castles of the Rhine. . . . Nor from the heather-clad hills where Scottish chiefs with claymore in one hand, pibroch in the other, charged across the Culloden Moors. . . . Nor did I spring, like Phoenix, from the ashes. . . .

"But I did spring from the good old county of Wetzel, where her teeming harvests leave no space for the upspringing of that obnoxious weed, ignorance (which I perceive flourishes hereabouts in abundance). I hail from the cloud-kissed hills of Wetzel, whose snow-capped peaks lift their shining front to greet the god of day whilst yet ye sluggards of the lowlands sleep, reclined on couches of inglorious ease. . . . Glorious Wetzel, whose sons are brave and daughters fair, and which today produces enough gas to light the world, oil to lubricate it, and brains enough to run it."

At the other end of the wordy stick was the mountain man of whom it was said with experienced tolerance—barely—"Gabe always was kindly dumb, but now that he's turned deef he can't hyear when to keep his mouth shut."

My intrigued acquaintance with a mainly self-taught back-country doctor began with hearing that he had an excellent collection of period kitchen furniture. So one morning when the mists of fall were wiping out the West Virginia hills as though perhaps they had been a mistake, I drove over to Roseby's Rock to see his antiques. By then anything of value had already been housed in a museum, but his sizable and cluttered log-cabin office that he used as his base of operation (sometimes literally) was a period piece in itself.

It was put up, Dr. Will told me, to accommodate the workmen when the B. and O. cut through that part of the mountains. And, he was proud to say, the log hotel was the only whistle stop between Baltimore and the Ohio River terminus that never once

lowered the Union flag in all four years of that coggled-up fray.
Dr. Will was getting on in years, but with a bridling vigor still,
and with reminder of the Civil War he plunged into an account
of how he happened to choose the medical profession. Whatever
else might be said of the rough old doctor, he was straight-
tongued. He knew only one way to call things, and that was as he
saw them.

"There's always been something blamed peculiar about my
family. The men have had one awful fear, scared to death of
bein' drafted. So when this ruckus started, my father gathered
up and enlisted. He went with the Union. He got back all right
and took up where he left off, as blacksmith. Now, in that day
and age a country blacksmith shop was kind of a club. Men
would bring a little poke of cold sweet potatoes and sit around
and talk, swap huntin' and fishin' yarns, or fight the war all over
again. My mother liked everything clean and neat, and had the
faculty of thinkin' anybody around the house should make themselves useful. So I used to slip off to the shop and listen to the
men's stories."

One of the war stories, although not the stuff of derring-do
that ordinarily excites a boy's imagination, nevertheless had its
significant effect. It revolved around a piece of civilian action at
the county seat.

"They were Northerners for fair down there, and when war
broke out, a committee of patriots called on Dr. James. They
opened the session by tryin' to make him raise his right hand and
swear to Almighty God that he was loyal to the Union.

"Now, James was a good doctor, the best-trained one in this
part of the country. There wasn't a thing in the world wrong
with him except that the first milk he ever drank had the taint of
royalty. He came from a fine old Richmond family and believed
to his soul in the Confederate cause. He refused to take the loyalty oath and the patriotic so-and-so's threw him in jail.

"One night a man rowed across the river from Ohio, ripped
and tore around town lookin' for Dr. James. It was late, but he
located a saloon that was still doin' business and the saloon
keeper told him the good townspeople had their doctor locked up.

So the man hustled around to the jail and got in to see Dr. James. He said his wife was terrible sick and would Doc go home with him right away. James said he'd be glad to under other circumstances, but he was afraid he couldn't get away just then.

"That Ohio man roused up the sheriff and give him a mighty argument. The sheriff pulled some clothes on and told James he could go if he'd promise to come back."

"And did he come back?"

"Well, not for five days, he didn't. When he got over there he found everybody in the family runnin' a fever and half the neighbors down sick. Then, when he wasn't needed no longer," said Dr. Will—dryly, from caustic experience—"the man who'd been in such a lather to fetch him forgot about carryin' him back. So Doc waded the river, swimmin' the channel. A skim of ice was floatin' and he reported in at the jailhouse about froze solid. The sheriff was shaken some. He told him to go home and get some dry clothes, and he could stay home if he'd take the oath of allegiance.

"Dr. James held fire a little, heart-torn about his duties. But it didn't take him so very long to know he couldn't take that oath, not and feel right in his conscience. And damned if those great defenders of the liberty didn't keep the only good doctor for miles around behind bars the whole war! Oh, they'd let him out now and again for a baby fracas or something, but it stuck in my craw, the way he was served."

The mist was clearing to show the hills growing sharp with color, and the clear-seeing countryman was finishing the story for himself. "One thing they didn't tell on him. He had guts. Doc James was a real man, he had hair on his chest. And when he went back to where he come from, I didn't fault him for it. But right then and there I made up my mind that when I grew to manhood, I'd make it up to him. That's why I went to West Liberty Normal School and took a year's medical course."

Thus began the career of a back-country practitioner who became fondly known for being, as one of his patients told me soberly by way of recommendation, "the best human doctor in three counties." Human, as opposed to horse.

You learn as you go.

On a summer afternoon, when shadows lying peacefully on a slope knew to lessen the scars, a Tennessee farmer's remembrance of the war's ending inclined toward the lyrical. He called to mind the sad tears that were shed for the soldiers sleeping under the fields where they fell, with only the heavens to weep for them there; and how poverty had paled the rosy cheek of the homefolk.

"But I was young and sorrow eased d'reckly. I started workin' our land again all day and went courtin' all night. Huskin' bees were great courtin' places. The lucky fellow that husked an ear of red corn got to kiss his sweetheart. I was wild as a buck in them days.

"Now, hit's no trouble for some women to be virtuous"—whether veering off into abstract rumination or speaking from personal experience, he didn't say. "They've got no more sexuality than a bedpost. The ones full of life and made for love deserve a mort of credit. They've got to try harder."

That succinct bit of most uncommon mountain male perceptiveness over with, he went on to say that his wife had been as sweet and pretty as a basket of speckled pups when he courted her. Amanda always wore some little ornament in her hair, a bright bow of wool thread or a posy. And she was the dancingest girl! A favorite play-party game with the young folks (they called it a game so the preachers wouldn't look down their noses) was Johnny Brown. If a fiddler wasn't around, they danced it to a song they sang while they joined hands and circled the gent in the middle.

"I've knowed that song from 'way back yonder.'" Obligingly he threw back his head and, tapping out the rhythm with a lean hand on his chair arm, he gave me a quavery sample of how light and gay it was, the song they danced to by fire shine and candle glow.

"Well done, well done," said Johnny Brown.
"Is this the road to London town?"

"Kneel ye down, oh kneel ye down,
And choose the fairest maid in town.
Kiss the one that you love best,
Kiss her now before she goes to rest."

"That's lovely!" I said, and meant it. It was growing easier by the minute to picture the dancing Amanda, too happy to think.

And then they were married. Everybody in the country got together and gave them a log rolling for their dwellin' house. And there they were, a young couple starting a new life in the old way.

"We didn't have nothin' much to start out with. We seen hard times, but we managed. My woman was stout"—fortunately, as the saga went on. "She done her share of axin' firewood out of the woods and packin' hit down steep places. We didn't have no animal to plow with, but we dredged out a clearin' and put in some grain. The summer ground was too cold to grow nothin' but flax, Irish potatoes and sometimes a little rye. Corn was our best-growin' grain, and every spring we'd put in a severe crop by hand and harvest hit the same way.

"We raised up our children to believe that if the family wanted food to eat, everybody had to he'p grow hit. All ten of our youngins as they come along—and they come fast and they come out even, five brothers and five sisters—could hoe as good as Amanda. Nary a one, though, could beat her when hit come to pitchin' hay—or manure, for that matter."

This was the best poor man's country there was, he said. In the fullness of time he got up some scrub sheep and cattle. He started out with a milk cow and bull. He paid for his stock by working in the iron mine. "That mine was opened up by a couple of men to keep from goin' to the war. North and South both were bad off for iron. When I worked there, I'd forge ax and hoe blades, harness gear, chains for loom pedals, and all like that.

"And the mountains were a joyful place for galax gathering," he said. "When the yaller leaves started droppin' from the timber, Amanda would go galaxin'. She'd gather up whole bunches of them green ground leaves, pack them down in damp moss, and save them ag'in a day a peddler come through. Peddlers were mostly Irish, you could discern it from their talk. My woman was a good hand at tradin', and she knew were the galax grew. Under a rock cliff she'd find the shiniest."

With the highlander's aptness for word portraiture, in a few low-toned strokes my afternoon host pictured the mountain woman's pleasure in earning a bit of pin money by gathering the heart-shaped leaves that grew singly. It was cool and dark, like twilight, along a trail of laurel roots and fallen logs, and the ferns waved high in the autumn wind. Where you had to bend low under the rhododendron to pick the glistening green galax, some of them touched by frost were turning a golden bronze. And then Amanda would linger over the awful decision of which piece of pretty calico to choose from among the wonders of the chatty peddler's pack—and eventually the leaves would go north by railroad to be sold at city florist prices as Christmas decorations.

Keeping the smokehouse filled, my withy Tennessee friend was saying, was no trouble at all. Many a morning he'd gone out before breakfast and shot down a deer. In the old days the woods were so thick with bears you couldn't grow a hog unless you stuck him up alongside the chimney at one side of the house. Even then, once in a while his woman would have to chop a b'ar out of the pen. He was a dear lover of hunting himself, and he'd started his boys out when they weren't much bigger than able to tag along after him. "Hain't no sweeter music than the bay of a dog arunnin' the fox"—unless it was the music of naked power made by Clark Schofield's overshot sawmill.

"First one in the country, a curiosity. Hit sawed up and down. The water come splashin' in from a wooden chute and hit that great big old wheel from overhead—hit her so hard, she turned. The wheel went round and round, and the saw went chuwhack, chuwhack. I could stand thar all day watchin' that sawmill work. Hit cut seven-eight hundred boards a day."

At recollection of his absorbed male interest that could keep him standing around the day long watching power at work, he pulled a plug of home-grown tobacco from a back jeans pocket, sliced off a piece, and offered politely, "Do you use? No? That's a fine thing. I wouldn't take to hit if I was you.

"At first Amanda couldn't get a grain of tobacco to grow, just little bitty sticks. Directly, though, she got the patch moved to a spot where the air wasn't so shaded and it grew first rate. There was nothing to curing it."

Should I ever care to try it, he told me his woman's method of curing the full-leaved stalks. "Hang hit in the shade till hit yallers, then in the sun till hit's well aged—as much as two days."

What with one thing and another, by nightfall, after his woman stuck a reaping knife in the barn wall, did the milking, and cleared the supper table, "she'd crawl under the quilts purty well played out." And then she played out altogether.

I never met the exemplary Amanda but I have seen her reflected a hundred times, a hundred ways. A young mother watches a sleeping child, smiling at him there against her breast, thinking of his future and her own warm present with him. . . . She stands in the background, unnoticed by a little boy sitting on a loose stone fence by the barn, following the flight of each swallow as it swoops upward. The woman has the eyes of a slow mind, but one fine dark brow lifts wistfully. . . . A woman about thirty, a little gray; that is all—nothing more. She walks down a slope with regular, even steps, her feet scarcely lifting from the ground; the unvarying level of her life. . . . The blue-veined hands of a weaver move to the rhythmic thud of loom pedals. She sends the wooden shuttles threading their delicate colors deftly through the intricate pattern of a Lee Surrender coverlet . . . an old lady, with a knotted beauty to her face, suggesting that she has learned to keep the tragedy and joy of her life knotted within her to quiet control.

The Amandas of the mountains might be summed up in the highland idiom that experience is the best teacher. "Bought wit is best, if you don't pay too dear for it."

Vendetta

*Frank James age 72 dide in Alabama Feb
20 1915 he ware bank rober him and
Jesy James and Bob Forde and Bob
Forde shot Jesy James in his own hous
for [re]ward of Thirty thosand dolars
Jesy ware hanin pitcher when shot he
ware won of gang for money*

WHEN Frank James was only a young drifter,
with a quicksilver laugh in his eyes and a style to the way his
striped trousers tucked into his high boots, occasionally he used
to visit the McCandlass family in Uncle Jake's Blue Ridge
neighborhood. The "neighborhood" was as far as you could see
from its loftiest points, the craggy peaks of Grandfather Mountain. On a clear day that was scarcely more than a hundred miles,
compassed by blue-gray mountains soft as a light scarf folded
carelessly by the winds. It was most unusual when a visitor
within those confines turned out so famously, or infamously, as
Frank James. Consequently, the rising career of the unrecon-
structed Southerner was followed with unwonted interest.

Some of the more conservative element who'd had a passing
acquaintance with young Frank had mistrusted him from the
start. Not straightforward, they said. "He looked shifty out of
his eyes." A few shook their heads darkly and predicted that they
were afraid the boy would get his killing before he got his
growth. As it happened, it was the killing of Frank's brother,
Jesse, that caused a neighborhood stir.

Izey Stamey was so incensed, he pounded the floor with his
cane. It wasn't the moral issue involved that he objected to. It

didn't rankle him a whit that a notorious outlaw had been murdered, or even shot in the back—poetic justice, more than likely.
What set old Izey to banging his cane was Bob Ford's incredibly
poor taste.

"Shockin', Fizey, shockin'," he sputtered to his wife Sophia.
"Imagine a fellow shootin' a man in his own house whilst eatin'
that man's salt!"

All the shocked Sophia could say for a fellow who so mis-
treated hospitality was that he plain didn't know how to do. And
personally, she added with fine disdain, "I wouldn't put myself
out to speak to the likes of him!"

The thrust of mountaineer pride doubtless was a factor in the
flash and outbreak of the blood feuds that marked a period of
sheer horror, especially in Kentucky and West Virginia. Men
whose spirited heritage claimed never to have been slaves to anyone became slaves to their own mortal passions. These vendettas
flared for various reasons, often trivial, but they definitely were
interfamily affairs.

The murderous and complicated Rowan County clan war
arose from a political argument between a Kentucky judge of
Northern sympathy and a Confederate governor. In the extreme
southeastern Kentucky mountains, the magnitude of the French-
Eversole war has largely been attributed to the lawless spirit of
the younger generation growing up in the disturbed wake of the
Civil War. The immediate cause for the gathering of armed
clansmen was the business rivalry of two merchants on the one-
street town of Hazard. Bloody Brethett's history of atrocity and
anarchy (whose proud cost included forty men slain in cold
blood between 1901 and 1902) began with the personal quarrel
of two officers in the same Federal regiment raised by the county.

Of all the internecine feuds that stained the mountains at the
turn of the century, none equaled the prolonged ferocity of the
Hatfield-McCoy war. Although the feud proper did not break out
until 1882, bad blood had been engendered during the Civil
War. Until then the two families had been friendly neighbors,
with intermarriages through their pioneer generations. They

were separated only by the rippling flow of Tug River, which marked a state boundary line in that section.

The break came when Anderson Hatfield, a Confederate captain in the Logan County Wildcats, organized an independent company of raiders, ostensibly to protect the West Virginia property of his widespread clan. On the Kentucky side of the river, Randolph McCoy, known as Old Randall, organized a similiar Federal force to protect his clan's site along Blackberry Branch.

Periodically the two forces invaded each other's territory, and in a clash toward the end of the highlanders' War Amongst Us, a McCoy raider was killed. From that moment on, the narrow rush of the Tug took on menacing meaning.

For brooding years thereafter, antagonism mounted over such seeming trifles as the ownership of a wild hog, though in those days falsely branding a hog corraled in the woods was comparable to cattle-stealing in the West. Even so, nothing of imminent tragedy occurred until a pair of star-crossed lovers walked into the roistering scene of an open-air election rally—together. Roseanna was a daughter of Old Randall, and Johnse the first-born son of the Hatfield chieftain, Devil Anse. Real trouble began when Roseanna's youngest and impetuous brother, Little Randall, loyally pulled a knife on a taunting Hatfield. In the subsequent free-for-all, fists and rocks gave place to gunplay; a fatal shot, flight, capture, the triple assassination at midnight in the Hatfield's Raccoon Hollow—and battle lines were drawn. Six years later the lines were still drawn—the battle of Grapevine Creek was the last serious fight between the two clans, although there were sporadic killings until 1911.

An eager oldster recently recounted for me the Hatfield-McCoy vendetta in zestful capsule. Man and boy he had lived in Enterprise, near Intercourse, he said, by way of assuring me he was a geographical authority on the subject. "It started over a wild hog and ended with a weddin', that's about the run of it."

While most of the blood feuds had their festering origin in the War of the Rebellion, in practice they all harked back to the participants' ancestral British Isles. Like the ancient Scots, the American feudists had a fierce clan fealty, and wild purposes of revenge were handed down from generation to generation—a sacred legacy of hatred.

Brutally savage though the Appalachian clan wars were, the Appalachian manner of bushwhack fighting was a slight refinement over the inherited code. In Jacobite Scotland and Tudor England, to take an enemy at disadvantage, whether he be Cardinal, Lord, or King, was considered "of all the arts Nature's chief masterpiece." At least our highland feudists gave the enemy warning—or so I gathered from an afternoon caller who rather alarmingly seemed to know whereof he spoke.

It was an afternoon in November, when there was the beginning of freezing to the ground, that hardening protection to soft surfaces. Already it was so cold the laurel and rhododendron leaves outside the windows were curled up tight. Against the lowering fire of a winter's sun, the smoke from a farmer's chimney across our front valley hung motionless, as though frozen short. All in all, a day of tenuous action, so I couldn't have been more surprised to answer an imperious clang of the front-door knocker and see my country doctor friend beaming at me.

His keen old eyes were a little watery and his face pinched rosy by the clear burn of quiet cold. Nevertheless, he arrived the personification of ideal mountain hardihood, a physical stamina that defies fatigue and weather. The aging Dr. Will was sans scorned topcoat. When I'd seen him before, his rumpled appearance had been almost as disreputable as his untidy office. But for this occasion he was dressed to the nines, as was a companion he had in tow, both looking uncomfortable in tightly buttoned suit coats. And the reason for Dr. Will's taking the roundabout bus trip to make a formal call was highly appreciated. Knowing my interest in local lore, he had dredged up a former acquaintance who was, he announced grandly, immediately they were safely inside, "a man who slept with Devil Anse Hatfield."

With that, the party was off. Sitting stiffly in the middle of the living-room love seat, the acquaintance, a Mr. Ransom, admitted modestly to Dr. Will's claim. When his business had taken him into the state's southern coal country, he had often stopped by the Hatfield place, had eaten at their plentiful table, and once, when all the boys were home and the house was crowded, he had shared the clan leader's bed.

"What did you think of Devil Anse?" I wondered curiously.

"Nicest man you ever saw," he assured me promptly. "Never killed anybody unless they insisted on it."

And that testimonial covered the classic Hatfield-McCoy feud, or as far as Mr. Ransom cared to comment. Quite plausibly, from forewarned habit, he was still adhering to a standard of mountain ethics. One does not inquire unnecessarily into another's private affairs—a restraint springing from instinctive tact and, in cases of family quarrels, the better part of healthy wisdom.

In any event, his statement of esteem was arresting, for it tallied with a respectful tone I had heard before. Other people who knew the heads of both clans, each with the brains, personal magnetism, and influence required of clan leaders, have generally conceded that normally the domineering Devil Anse and more reserved Old Randall were as neighborly, honest, thrifty, and obliging men as ever drew the breath of life.

Mr. Ransom was busily adjusting his steel-rimmed glasses that roamed around over his bony nose, preparatory to branching out into other feuds. Just because two great Generals in the low-lands, Lee and Grant, agreed to shake hands, so to speak, was no reason why a mountain man named Dan'el felt any call to follow suit with his erstwhile friend Claude.

Dr. Will interposed brightly that he knew a Claude. Mr. Ransom favored him with a doubtful peer. The Claude he was talking about got pistol shot. Dr. Will had never heard of him.

Mr. Ransom went on calmly to say the two men had not been friends for some time, not since a kin of Dan'el's gut shot Claude's cousin, and the cousin's last words to the neighbors who found him were not to bother looking for the fellow who plugged him, he was dead.

"A year later they met by accident. One day when Dan'el was at the sawmill, who should come riding up the creek but Claude. Dan'el didn't feel to stir up the family ruckus, so when Claude pulled in alongside and made out he was pleased to see him, Dan'el made out he was pleased to hear it. They talked a little bit but neither of them would pin themselves down to anything until Claude suggested, 'Let's make up our quarrel and shake hands.' Dan'el said he was willing to make up the quarrel, but he wouldn't shake hands."

"Why not?" I asked.

"Because," said Mr. Ransom reasonably, "Dan'el suspicioned Claude of shakin' with his right hand and shootin' with his left. Claude got mad and left quicker than he come. The last Dan'el ever saw of him, he was layin' the whip to his horse and splashin' downstream. But sometime later I read in the paper about a peculiar duel that took place on a street in Pikeville. Two men met, shook hands, and killed each other. Claude had met another left-handed shooter."

"They have a strange code of honor," continued Mr. Ransom, talking more to Dr. Will slumped in his chair across the room than to me sitting off to one side. Warming to his subject, the study he had made of settling grudges by the gun, he unbuttoned his coat to a brace of striped suspenders he wore long. "They never kill anybody without warnin'. It may just be that one man says to another, 'I'll get you!' But that's fair warning for the other fellow to be on his guard from then on—sleepin', eatin', or lookin' out his door to see what kind of day it is. Any place, any time.

"And another strange thing," giving another adjustment to his rambling spectacles, "aimin' at a target and at a man are altogether different. I can always hit the target but I can't always hit the man, especially if he's shootin' at me."

"Well now," said Dr. Will, straightening determinedly. Not to be left out of the conversation entirely, not he who was given to carrying it, he adopted a scientific viewpoint. "A sure-fire aim is all right but that ain't the whole of it. There's some psychology mixed in. It stands to reason that the man who knows he's goin' to kill somebody has that instant's advantage over the other fellow who hasn't quite made up his mind yet."

So Dr. Will had the last word after all.

Moonshine

Jery Kiney age 91 june 25 1913 ware
farmer & made whisky by 100 galons
drank licker his days never ware drunk
in his days

J ERY KINEY was well known in North Carolina
legal circles. He was a moonshiner of parts. In the last twenty
years of his blockading activities he had been called up before
nearly every session of Circuit Court. At each hearing he pleaded
guilty and accepted his jail sentence without a murmur. While
he did not see eye to eye with the law, he was an agreeable sort
and the authorities tended to be lenient. If his sentence was a
twelve-month tenure, he usually came out looking as though he
had wintered well. In the spring and fall he was allowed to go
home and tend his crops. No bond was ever asked or given, except his word. And he always came back, bringing his own
blanket roll.

On his seventieth birthday, up before Judge Dick, he told the
Judge privately, "You've got a case against me you don't know
about and couldn't prove. But I'll tell you man to man that right
now I've got three stills a-runnin' back yonder on Gingercake
Mountain. If you'll dismiss this case, I promise you that I'll get
rid of them stills in three months and never knowingly go where
one is." The Judge dismissed the case and Jery kept his promise.

Even as a lawbreaker from the government's point of view,
Jery Kiney stood for what is considered a cardinal virtue by the
southern highlanders: honesty. Born to freedom within, nobody

could make them agree with something they did not believe was true. They simply did not believe that distilling the grain of their own fields and the fruit of their own orchards was crime. And they never had.

The mountaineers' knack for distilling was primarily part of the transit of Old World skills and customs. Irish ancestors had made a convivial whiskey from their most plentiful crop, potatoes. Scotch forebears had brewed a whiskey from their rye. The liquor of the British Isles had been distilled in little pots, called poteens by the Irish—"enough for every man and his neighbor" and as intrinsic a domestic industry as hearth-baked bread. For the transplanted American highlanders, pot-stilling their fruit and grain, both for medicine and pleasure, was as basic an agricultural activity as raising flax to be spun into linen thread for clothing. Corn was their most staple food crop; corn liquor, sold by saddle bag or pack horse, their most marketable commodity.

Albert Gallatin, later Jefferson's distinguished Secretary of the Treasury, being an Appalachian farm owner and knowing the tortuous mountain roads, had defended the practice. "We have no means of bringing the produce of our lands to sale either in grain or meal. We are therefore distillers through necessity, not choice, that we may comprehend the greatest value in the smallest size and weight. The inhabitants of the eastern side of the mountains can dispose of their grain without the additional labor of distillation at a higher price than we can after we dispose that labor upon it." Thomas Jefferson, too, had vigorously opposed the tax levied after the Revolutionary War and, when he became President, had it repealed.

After the Civil War there was no Gallatin, no Jefferson, no financier-statesman, no friend at all in Federal officialdom to speak up in behalf of the small distiller.

The formalities of peace were scarcely over when the financial drain of the war demanded increased revenue. The Federal tax on spiritous liquors that had started at twenty cents a gallon in 1862 and risen to sixty cents in 1864 suddenly leaped to an unheard-of excise of two dollars a gallon. This was a staggering blow to the main cash source of a disaster-struck, land-poor mountain economy trying to get back on its own shaky feet.

Not every mountain farmer fell into the distilling category, of course. But the memory of the mountains is long. The majority of Blue Ridge people had an ingrained loathing of the word "excise," which they defined as Dr. Johnson did: "A hateful tax levied upon commodities, and adjudged not by common judges of property, but by wretches hired by those to whom excise is paid."

Moreover, if there was one thing every sovereign-souled highlander heartily agreed upon, it was an active dislike of having his thinking dictated, in war or peace. As the small distillers saw the revenue matter, they stubbornly contended that what a farmer did with his own hard-grown crops was his business, and none of Washington's. Law-abiding mountain citizens or those who might personally disapprove of drinking nevertheless were thoroughly in accord with this contention. It was taxation without representation all over again. As a bridling Lost River farmer put it, "We'd be as well off farin' under a King!" They had rebelled then, and they rebelled now. "A state of healthy public opinion," is how a baffled U.S. Commissioner reported the clandestine revolt.

In a sense, the unnamed revolt was another turn of the historic wheel, back to the British Isles and their progenitors who had felt a greater fealty to clan than to government. In America it brought the term "moonshine" into being, meaning liquor made under cover of darkness, preferably when wind-blown clouds made the light of the moon uncertain. Notwithstanding, rifles readied, pot stillers moved their crudely contrived equipment farther back into "the jaws of the hills" and imperturbably continued to harvest a goodly portion of their crops by the jug in order to get cash money to pay their property tax—a logic lost on the frustrated Department of Internal Revenue.

This is the era that introduced Jery Kiney to the North Carolina legal circles, although it was well known by the silent mountains he'd been making liquor for years before he was caught.

The fact that his final compliance with the law was by his own volition, and on his terms, indicated that the government was still having its difficulties with the independent mountaineers.

As for enjoying their homemade beverages, devout Scotch-Irish Presbyterians, if so inclined, could follow with a perfectly clear conscience the Biblical admonition: "Give strong drink unto him that is ready to perish, and wine unto those with a heavy heart." The circumspect of any sect might choose to abide by the text: "It is not for Kings to drink wine, nor princes strong drink" —which left quite a leeway for the cup of cheer. And on the self-dependent frontier there was more truth than poetry to Timothy's advice regarding using "a little wine for thy stomach's sake and thine oft infirmities."

The propensity for endorsing whatever appealed to them with scriptural quotations could even produce a verse that satisfactorily sanctioned the moonshine trade: ". . . wine maketh merry, but money answereth all things." Transmitted to the North Carolina idiom of Uncle Walt Clark, speaking from practical farming experience when he was a young man and first married, "Whiskey was a common man's best money crop."

Being a man of brawn, not books, probably he had never heard of the Honorable Albert Gallatin, nor his stately defense of Appalachian farmers who marketed their produce in distillate form as an economic necessity. Yet here Uncle Walt was, his splint-bottomed chair tilted back against the sunny side of his house, squinting reminiscently into a September morning of the 1930's and putting forth virtually the same argument.

Uncle Walt was well stricken in years but apparently with enough virility left for me to wonder vaguely why, when I used to turn in at his front walk, I often glimpsed a skirted figure disappearing into the limbo from his back door. Be that as it may, the old rapscallion was a gold mine of miscellaneous information, such as Sam Carpenter's having the first grist mill in the country. It was at the head of Cranberry Creek, and you could get your corn ground there on shares, at a tenth of a bushel. But the mill was twelve miles away, "too fur a piece to haul a sled load of corn every time you wanted a dab of meal."

"In the early days," Uncle Walt said, "we had no roads, least-wise the words of a wagon driver warn't fitten for the air he was usin' up."

Then he took an adverse line of reasoning. Moonshining was a mort of trouble, and risky. The total output of whiskey might be by the "100 gallons," but a 25-gallon still was the average, so a man could pick it up and carry it around—a precautionary meas-ure should it suddenly become prudent to move to another loca-tion.

Also, it was customary to have several stills running concur-rently, as Jery Kiney had on Gingercake. Uncle Walt had been to the crags of Gingercake many times, he said. It was a great still place, hard to get to, and hard work once there. Scrabbling around from one hidden spot to another, stumbling through laurel slicks by shadowy moonlight, or barking your shins in rock holes on nights black as the inside of your hat could get tiresome. Then, you had to keep the pots boiling just so. A kettle fired by charcoal was safest, because it didn't send up telltale smoke drifts. After you'd cracked your corn, brewed it into a sour mash, run the vapors a couple of times through condensing coils cooled by spring water, you weren't half done. The liquor had to be poured into small kegs, or jugs strapped together, something a man could shoulder down a narrow trail while keep-ing a sharp eye out for ambush.

Even if you made it down off the mountain with your liquor before a Revenuer got it—and you never came or went over the same trail—a stout pack horse could only carry about sixteen gallons a trip. When roads got some better, a blockader could hide more of his ware in kegs under a wagon load of apples and fodder. But the nearest market to amount to anything was likely to be a two- or three-day journey—longer, if you broke an axle. And in strange country—a railroad stop or lumber camp—there was no telling whether the fellow who came to buy was a cus-tomer or an agent.

All in all, it was Uncle Walt's opinion that Jery Kiney was only using the brains the good Lord gave him when he quit blockad-ing, "tuk to religion and had peace spoke to his never-dyin' soul."

He did grant, though, with a broad wink, "The price of corn went up after they put a law out a'gin hit."

Conversely, as the margin of profit on bootleg whiskey rose, so did the baneful vigilance of informers. The common run of informers—pretended friends, or someone taking out a personal jealousy under guise of authority—was universally despised and spoken of with emphatic contempt. "Worthless old cuss, mean as a snake, too lazy to work for an honest livin' himself; crawly old varmint, sneakin' off to the law just to get him enough money to get pesky drunk on," are some of the credit lines.

Sometimes, though, the informer was a worried wife or mother, tired of having her heart jump with fear every time she heard a woods sound that wasn't the wind fingering the leaves. And in the way that concern can veer off unexpectedly into the clear decision of cold anger, she went to a deputy.

Trouble among the moonshiners themselves was most apt to flare when tired and edgy men were making a division of the final runoff. One might claim that his should be the larger share because he furnished the most raw material, and his partner argue that he did most of the work. Usually before an argument reached the in-fighting stage, a trusted third man was selected to act as arbitrator.

Such a man was Isaac Johnston. He was a staunch prohibitionist, a good man, respected for speaking his mind and meaning what he said. Uncle Ike would come immediately when summoned, and never accepted any payment for negotiating a settlement. He merely was being a civic-minded citizen with a real interest in keeping the peace. Should reasoning fail, he was a master at tension-releasing humor. Once a dispute reached an ominous level when one moonshiner, soft of voice and cold of eye, asked another how he'd like to get thrashed till he'd wish he were "absolent from his broken body." Retorted his partner, "You'll play Hell!" Uncle Ike turned toward him, quizzical brows raised. "Begone! I be an older man than you be, and I've never seen that game played yet." Both combatants stared at him and grinned sheepishly. And that was that.

"Well," said Uncle Walt, bringing his tilted chair down to the porch floor with a thud, "I like to forgot what I was fixin' to tell you!"

What he'd had in mind was an enthusiastic recipe for johnny-cake. By way of setting the scene for the corn-bread cookout, he said, "Hit don't differ whether thar's a grist mill handy. The best meal for johnnycake, you grit yourself. Just dig a trench out of doors," he recommended as the starting process, "and roll logs into hit to burn. After the fire has died down, stick two locust forks in the ground, one at each end of the trench. Lay a board scaffolding between the forks, lay yore ears of corn on hit, and dry them slow over the embers. Then grit the dried corn with a piece of cut tin, make hit into a batter, roll hit in damp leaves, rake a hole in the ashes, and bake. Of all the good eatin' I ever eat, that was the wonderfulest!

"Or you could," he amended considerately, "bake hit on the hearth in a covered iron pot. Put hot coals on top and under-neath, and hit'll bake you sweet, crusty bread."

His second wife had found that a heap sight convenienter, he said, jerking a horny hand toward the open front door. Not a pretentious old house, but substantial, with its wide center hall ending with a flight of stairs leading to the second floor, and all of it fairly shrieking for care in the frank light of day. But a side glance into the duskiness of a room to the right of the entrance hall showed the nostalgic glow of a fire burning down to inter-mittent green-gold flames. An iron rack on either side of the hearth was hung with big, smoke-blackened pots. And for a mo-ment his world-sagged face, etched with lines not put there alto-gether by hard work, was sad.

Then he brightened again, as mention of his second wife brought reminder that she'd had the first pair of boughten shoes ever seen up that way. She had ridden thirty miles on horseback to get her button shoes. She bought them to be married in. "I went to my weddin' in style too, wearin' a checked suit of home-spun and ridin' a wild animal"—a high-stepping horse.

"She was a purty woman, and I'd do anything for a purty woman. I was aimin' to be mannerly for her and not frolic too much. A weddin' didn't happen very often in those days and when it did, everybody in the country gathered for it. They come from every direction, on horseback, on foot, some by oxteam and wagon. It was all set for a Saturday night—her folks had even got in a preacher." And the men were all set to give him a sort of bachelor's party before the preacher said the words, "Stand, jine hands, hitched."

"Everybody made up their fruit and corn then and didn't think nothin' about it. And for the infair the men had got in a lot of whiskey to wish me well and a helluva time. It was a fine evenin'. A moon was risin' low, hangin' yaller riper and ready to be picked. But afore I knowed it, I was wool-gatherin'—all the wool in the fields, by gollies. Of all the foolish shines I ever cut, that was the most unthoughted."

Even yet, just remembering, he gave a wry scratch to his iron-gray hair bristling up through the crown of his battered straw hat. "I should have denoted that drunk was comin' on, because that's when I always got shy." So the second-time-around groom spent his wedding night in the hay mow.

Uncle Walt has long since gone to his reward. But his moonshine and moonlight reveries stay near, part of a mountain September, and days that say, look at those hills, those ash-blond and green corn hills, all quiet and fresh in the morning sun.

And only in a recent spring, when everywhere you turned or looked our hills were a world of blossoming apple trees, I heard of a West Virginia moonshiner giving a bit of individual flare to the trade. A lawyer whose practice is in the South Branch of the Potomac Valley told me with amusement about a case he had lost the week before. It had a reminiscent ring, for his client bore a character resemblance to North Carolina's Jery Kiney, up to a point. He admitted truthfully to the liquor-traffic charge and paid his fine without demur. An upright judge accepted the mountain man's word as being as good as his bond when he promised never again to make, sell, or drink whiskey. There the story digresses. After the case was dismissed, the canny hillman told his lawyer, "The judge didn't say one damned word about applejack! And I've got five gallons at home, just waitin' to sell or celebrate."

Moreover, he was an habitual consumer of his own product. Every night after supper he took a wine bottle of apple brandy from a kitchen shelf and poured himself a searing cup, which he laced with sugar.

Repeatedly in Uncle Jake Carpenter's diary of Blue Ridge life and death he notes that such and such a man made whiskey by the gallons. With almost equal frequency the factual entry states that the distiller never was "drunk in his days," or "never had a drunk boy in family"; or somebody "got snake bit but brandy cured it" or, as in one lamentable instance, death came because "no brandy could be got."

Although there have been scandalizing exceptions, especially during the clan wars, the southern mountain people as a class have long been noted for being remarkably temperate. Those who indulge, whether for health or spirit, seldom go on sprees. Rather, they are moderate drinkers, on the order of a steady drop on a rainy day. They have their little niceties, as reported of a man named Bish in the Smoke Hole district, although, compared to his cousin Squire Thomas, Bish was only a footnote of a man.

The squire had a hard high frame, an uneven swagger of mustache, and a powerful way about him. He appointed himself Justice of the Peace every four years and nothing was ever said. He could neither read nor write, but when called upon to perform some function of his office, he explained that he didn't keep records because he didn't want nosy strangers going over his books.

Yet the squire was progressive, in his fashion, and early one spring he ordered a modern hand plow through a store in Franklin. He had a field with a southern exposure that soon would be ready to cultivate, but the Smoke Hole road was so poor, all ice and mud, even a horse couldn't drag an iron plow through the March muck. So, in the gray dawn of an impatient morning, the squire set off for town on foot. It was deep night before he sloshed in home.

Whether he ate too much supper, or whether his emotional disturbance was caused by his wife Pyrene not appreciating the rarity of the plow he had sent away for and she would have to struggle with, the squire went to bed with a distressed stomach.

His churning innards might have been caused, of course, by his eating his cold-snack supper when he was tired. He had packed that plow on his back for seventeen miles. It weighed seventy pounds if it weighed an ounce, and toward the end he'd had to set it down every half mile or so.

At any rate, when he wakened next morning and pulled his boots on, he was in bad humor. He was in such a grum sulk his muscles ached for man-sized physical labor. In that mood he stalked from the house and started to clean out the cowshed. He might have gone on heaving heavy forkfuls of wet manure till noontime, had not his cousin Bish appeared to ask him a question regarding the law.

"Why didn't you holler?" growled the squire in greeting. "Never go into a man's yard without hollerin'." Then, relenting a little, "I don't feel to do any legal talkin', Bish. I'm totin' a misery." At his cousin's concerned blink through the doorway, the squire, in woeful need to confide in somebody, jammed his pitchfork into a steaming pile, clumped on outside, and invited, "Cousin Bish, find yourself a downlog and set. I want to tell you my troubles." He sat down on the woodpile and Bish obligingly took a seat on the chopping block.

"A woman," began the squire broodingly, "is a cross between animal nature and human. Always has been. But lately Pyrene's been a-gettin' uppity on me. Last night I et something at my own table that danged nigh p'isoned me. And when I got in the bed, I said, 'Pyrene, I've got the bellyache.' And what do you think that woman done?" he demanded.

"What?"

"She said, 'Now, ain't that a shame,' turned her back on me, and went to sleep!" The squire was still flabbergasted.

Bish spat soberly off to the side. "That's serious. Let the word get around that yore woman's a-gettin' notions and not a man in the district will be able to do a thing at home."

"Bish," roared the squire disconsolately, "step up to the still with me. Back under that thar rock cliff I've got a keg of the first licker I ever made."

Bish's throat went suddenly dry.

"That licker," bellowed the squire, clambering down from the woodpile, "is thick as winter honey and the same color."

His cousin came up off the chopping block, although he said doubtfully, "Don't know as I ever drank with a man afore he got his shirt on of a mornin'."

"Well, then, tell you what you do," the squire was striding along in fine fettle now. "You take yore tinful, and go around t'other side the mountain with hit."

Bathsheba of Roseby Rock

George Frank age 45 dide July 15 1915
he has been veri bad feler had got better

I never knew what to expect of Dr. Will, except the unexpected. The roughhewn country doctor was getting on, but age seemed only to sharpen his native instinct for inquiry and his talent for shrewd observation that sparked anything he cared to talk about—and he was a talker!

When last I saw him in the anachronism of his log office at Roseby Rock, the day was hard and still. A late March snow, flat flakes that stick to things, had outlined with amazing exactness one side of every branching tree along his creek. There was just enough stir to the air for one harsh leaf to go rattling all by itself down the stony path to his door. I'd driven over the back hill road to his valley, hoping to hear more of the trenchantly remembered Civil War stories he'd listened to as a boy in his father's blacksmith shop. But from the abstracted way he poked up a coal fire till the pot-bellied stove glowed red, and from his opening conversational remark, obviously his questing mind was bent on a more cosmic struggle.

"What is this old world all about?" There were loose pouches under his eyes where the rogue and the philosopher lived by turns, but there was nothing loose to the look he was giving a problem that evidently was becoming an obsession with his advancing years. Mainly self-taught in his practice, the unkempt old doctor never had been allowed professionally inside the sterile halls of a modern hospital. Just the same, he had brought his share of lives into the world, often by the light of a shivering hatful of fire—and sometimes wondered why.

"Blackstone says that life is the period of existence between birth and death, which is just about as clear and lucid as a West Virginia mudhole." He gave a dissatisfied slam to the iron stove door, slouched into his swivel chair behind a dusty and book-littered desk, and pursued his pondering.

"I've read the Koran, the Book of Mormon too. But as I see it, the best record we've got is all mixed up in the Old Testament—" and he waved a fairly clean hand over a big Bible spread open before him.

Knowing from experience that the old hillman went on the principle, "plain talk is best understood," I braced myself. Perhaps because his reading glasses happened to be lying on that page, he proceeded to rock me to the heels by a rapid-fire hillside version of King David's sin against Uriah. While he frankly took scampish glee in being shocking, particularly in trying me out at the beginning, he was not being heretical—far from it, as subsequently developed.

Certainly his hillside history of the King's driving force lost none of the very human inconsistencies that make David one of the fundamentally real figures in all ancient history. The Bathsheba episode, which has fascinated many another transcriber, was, in the old country doctor's version, about as basic as you could get. By an incisive combination of vintage army slang and mountain vernacular he told it strictly from the man-woman angle and launched into it with a bang.

"David the King, that sweet singer of psalms, the pious old hypocrite." And up came a quickly restraining flat of a hand, forestalling any stuffy demur. "Now, don't get me wrong. Those psalms are through and through all right. It's Davey the man I'm talkin' about. And what I'm tellin' you is the gospel truth."

It probably was, essentially. So I settled back in a very old wooden chair across the desk from him and prepared to listen without interruption to a very old story, for plainly my friend was telling it with intent. Having made sure of my attention by his alerting start, I merely was a sounding board for the transposed epic he took racing along toward some silent search of his own.

"After David got to be head of the whole push, one night he was prancin' around on his palace rooftop, with a sergeant trottin' along behind swattin' mosquitoes, when derned if he didn't look down and see a woman stripped stark naked takin' a bath in his lily pond. 'Who's the doll?' The orderly didn't answer, gettin' an eyeful himself. So David asked again, 'Who is that woman?' The orderly snapped to and said, 'That's Mrs. Uriah.' 'Well, go get her,' said David. 'I'd like to meet her.'

"Captain Uriah was away. He was out fightin' the Philistines. Davey was a fast worker, and he slept with Mrs. Uriah that same first night. In due season Beth said, 'David, there's something I've got to talk to you about. I didn't come around last month.'" Another quick glance at my involuntarily widened eyes, and for a sedate instant Dr. Will reverted to the original text. "'I am with child.'

"'Hell's bells!' said David. 'Why did this have to happen to me right now when I've got all these wars on my hands?' But he studied over it and said, 'Beth, I'll just send a fellow after Uriah to come home for a furlough.' So he sent a runner after Uriah, only naturally the Captain reported in first to headquarters. David asked him how the war was goin' and all that, then said, 'Uriah, you go on along home and get washed up. I'll send a mess of vittles over to the house and you and Beth have a good time.'

"But on his way, Uriah got to thinkin' about his buddies raw-hidin' it back in the trenches and decided he couldn't enjoy a comfortable bed. He said to himself, 'That would be an unsoldiery thing to do. I'll be switched if I wouldn't feel better just campin' outside the King's gates.'

"Next mornin' Beth come sneakin' in the back door and said, 'Davey, Uriah never come in home last night.' 'Well Lord God, ain't that awful,' said David. 'I'll try again.' So that evenin' he had Uriah eat and drink with him and got him pretty well tanked up. Then he said, 'Now, Uriah, Beth's been kinda lonesome. She's got a good bed over there and I want you to go to sleep in it tonight.'"

"Well, Uriah started out, feelin' better about the idea since it was orders from the King, only he stopped off at the barracks to see some of his buddies and got in an all-night poker game.

"Next mornin' Beth come in worried. 'David, do you think Uriah suspects? Is that why he don't come home?' David didn't know, but things were gettin' drastic. He sent Uriah back to the army, with a note to his Colonel. The note ordered a charge against a walled city, with Captain Uriah leadin' the charge. 'And when you get him up there,' David wrote the Colonel, 'the rest of you fellows fall back and let the Philistines take care of Uriah.' Well, the Philistine women took a hand in that battle, got to heavin' bedchambers and millstones over the wall, and one of them felled the Captain.

"David, bein' the good religious man he was, wrote a fine obituary for Uriah. He give it out that in the heat of engagement a valiant soldier had been killed, and had him buried with all the honors of war. Beth went into mournin', then told David he'd better dig up a preacher before the neighbors started talkin'.

"The Lord was none too pleased with the King's sinful ways and sent word to say so. David admitted he'd done wrong and deserved his punishment. But eygoddy, when the baby come and took bad sick, Davey threw an awful tear. He bellyached around, got himself done up in burlap and ashes, laid out on the ground, and was goin' to starve himself to death. That little baby wasn't long for this world, but a Prophet told the King his sin was taken away too—all was forgiven. So Davey chirked up and had himself a good feed."

Thus far, by and large, Dr. Will had offered the story for what it was worth, with no attempt at personal evaluation. But suddenly he broke it off, a steely glint in eyes and voice, and simply glared at me.

"Now, wasn't that one hell of a raw deal for poor old Uriah?" he demanded indignantly.

For startled want of better answer, I conceded that he had a point. I didn't know exactly what kind of point, but anyway he had one. Somewhat mollified, he roughed his white hair in honest perplexity.

"There's hitch in it somewhere. If the Lord's omnipotent, what's the Devil doin' runnin' a joint establishment?"

The only thing I could be sure of right then, from a lift of wind making a clatter in a tree branch outside the window, was the wisdom of starting home before the unpredictable March day brewed trouble. Dr. Will agreed that he wouldn't be surprised but what it was blowin' up a stormy spell and saw me to the door. For a moment he paused silently on the wide threshold, looking out, his old gaze clearing.

It was a clear-cut black and white day, dark trees growing restive under their burden of snow. So much black and white, a forest of it, yet you could still get confused—until you had need to be confronted by a forest of oak and elm and pine, each quite different from the other, yet each perfect in itself. As a whole it afforded a vision as inexplicable as the power of great music. What the country-wise doctor was seeing clearly did not come from anything he had read. He spoke out from what was most profound in him, a seeking for certainty in something more mysterious than his own comprehension.

"I can't rightly name it, but we're not creatures of chance. There's some divine plan"—inconclusive, but his highest contribution to the enigma that so obsessed him. Then he coughed elaborately, to be brusque. "Well, go on. Get goin' before I start analyzin' myself, and that would puzzle you and me both."

Immediately I stepped in our own hilltop door, while his David and Bathsheba story was still fresh in mind, I checked it with the King James version. The sceptered wording of the written record was totally lacking in his idiomatic treatment, of course, but fact for eventful fact, his account tallied right down the elemental line with the Biblical text. A few of its classic details, shocking even by today's standards, the gruff old hillman had tactfully omitted.

And after all it did not storm that day, nor for days. There was only the whip of the wind on the bare trees, the whip of life on the shining limbs of budding branches—and the sound they made was the ecstatic sound of the pain of growing. Nothing is ever static in the hills.

Shift of Sun and Shadow

Avery Bush age 74 dide apr 5 1916
ware farmer veri good nebor he sed
what he thot

THE night's rain brought shafts of sun to the early April morning, and a wind I couldn't quite place. It was something like the first warm one that blows over the snow, and something like a sea wind. And, strangely, it seemed to have daisies blowing in it. I was starting for a walk down a lane that wanders along the southern crest of our front valley. It leads to the far edge of a ridge, and from there there's never any telling—it all depends on your mood, your companion, or the quality of the mist. On its way it passes through a narrow strip of upland farm. A familiar lane, but each time different.

This morning it was rough, mud cracked with a late winter breaking up, and from ahead came the sound of plowing. "Whoa, whoa, gee now, whoa, haw"—a crooning of man to his beast and the clank of harness. The farmer was preparing a garden patch beside a house built sturdily by some far-seeing early settler. Built long and close to the ground, graced by a pillared porch, it looks the sort of house Washington might have been born in had he been poorer.

"Whoa!" The farmer had reached the end of a furrow as I came alongside and called, "Nice day!"

Mr. Flannigan held his mule in check and paused straddle-footed behind his plow while he considered his answer. He looked down at my muddy boots, then up through the clear blue air to one drifting pink cloud, and struck a balance.

"Nice day overhead," he granted, a shy twinkle in his eyes.

Some such exchange was the extent of conversation with our neighbor, although we often used his lane. It was a favorite starting place for going with the children to gather the spring wildflowers that carpeted the valley woods below his farm. Alone or with weekend friends my husband and I walked it when clean winter was in one sharp breathful, and when the rustle of wind in the high field grasses of fall was only a touch of the strength it had in store. Occasionally when the air was soft-winded, not soft like the cheek of youth but soft as the worn red shawl around her shoulders, we used to see the farmer's wife sitting on the porch. She would lift a hand in greeting as we passed. That was all.

Then, late on an August afternoon, as I was driving home from town, at the top of a hill commanded by a white-steepled church with narrow pointed windows like praying hands, there was Mr. Flannigan toiling down out of the cemetery carrying a shovel. He had aged; stooped tired at the end of the day.

"Well, hello, Mr. Flannigan! How are you?"

"About half," he admitted as he accepted my offer of a ride. The day was hot and he was sweaty. But after the countless times he had made us feel welcome to use his lane, giving him a short ride home seemed a very small thing to do. Somewhat surprisingly, our reticent neighbor left few conversational gaps to fill as we drove on over the hill road home. He asked interestedly about the family, glad to hear they were well and busy. As for himself, he said he wasn't much at farming these days. He just kept a few chickens and pigs, and a cow. But the church had made him custodian of the cemetery. It gave him something to do and he liked the work.

His handiwork was evident in the well-kept grassy knoll with its pleasantly informal planting of gleaming-leafed rhododendron and old-fashioned peony clumps. It was a pretty little graveyard and it had a lovely view. I've often idly wondered why the country dead invariably have the finest views—a subject Mr. Flannigan and I did not go into.

He was saying he liked keeping the cemetery up because some

of his folks were buried there. And, he added with a shy chuckle, about the best place to see his friends any more was at a funeral. The first funeral he'd ever helped with had been his grandfather's. "Now, *that* was a nice burial," he said enthusiastically.

He remembered how his grandfather—he was long-minded—had said, "Up in the barn loft I've got some poplar boards all cut to size. Make them into my coffin." The young Mr. Flannigan hadn't thought too highly of the idea. "La, I never made a man's coffin!" But his grandfather had put it to him fair and square. "Did you ever ask me anything I denied you?" No-o. "Then don't deny me this." Then he said to young Mr. Flannigan's wife, "You drape the outside with black, and line the inside with white muslin. And both of you see to it that I get a burial as would suit a veteran of the Eighty-fifth West Virginia."

From the tenor of grandfather, I assumed he got his burial as directed. And he did. As Mr. Flannigan assured me sincerely, "It would have pleasured him."

The pulpit of the hilltop church—only then it was a log church house—happened to be vacant when the planned-for ending came. But Mr. Flannigan rode down to Little Grave Creek and asked a man whose father had been in the same Union regiment to give the funeral oration.

"You couldn't rightly call him a preacher, but he was a knowin' man. He said some mighty nice words over Grandpa, then he give him the three-gun salute. That idea started a long time back," he explained. "They got it goin' around that if they called a man's name three times and he didn't answer, he was dead."

Wherefore the power of this countryman in dirty workclothes, an earth-smeared shovel in his hand? But it was there, attracting you, holding you. It held me wondering when we came to his turnoff and he did not start walking on down his lane at once. He stood in the roadside weeds by the car, his thoughts seemingly far off. He stood as though it was enough to watch the quiet deepness of cloud shadows moving across the valley into upland sun. When he did turn back, it was with a smile of almost child-like sweetness in his country eyes accustomed to the long look. And instead of the usual thanks-for-the-ride, he resorted to a quotation.

" 'Cast your bread upon the waters,' " he began the familiar text with a slight lift of gentle voice, and finished it on a surge of sheer improvising. "Joyously watch it go, and it will come back to you a hundredfold. I thank you."

And our neighbor was gone. Needless to say, his exultant transcription of Ecclesiastes took me sailing on up around the curve of our own drive. In his pastoral way, our farmer neighbor bespoke a very special quality of the Appalachian right to religious freedom. It was a personal thing, and person to person.

You may hear it expressed in a spirit of cosmic sympathy with the Almighty, as a Kentucky woman said of June's tenderness, "Even the Lord now and then has to take out from the sorry side of things, and make Himself a pretty day just to enjoy."

Much of mountain community life revolved around the church, whether it was a Union meeting held in the open air or within sanctuary walls laid up by the parish men. For the minister to be invited to share Sunday dinner with some family of his congregation was standard procedure, and bustling on the women's part who put forth their best. Alack a day, often the impoverished parson barely put food on his own family's table, paid as he was for keeping his flock from skidding into perdition by farm produce given by people as poor as he.

In prosperous Colonial days, the preacher was apt to be well paid in the common commodity of the time, homemade liquor, until fire-and-brimstone revivalists started denouncing drink as "the scum of Hell"—a fair enough description if the whiskey wasn't "well aged." As an experienced hillman said appreciatively of a hopeful political candidate's 114-proof Kentucky bourbon, "Must be a month or so old, ain't it?"

Naturally, many a mountaineer has never been known to darken a church door. On the other hand, the faithful have never been inclined merely to turn up dutifully on Sunday and sit listening to what the preacher had, or had not, to say.

I remember a summer when a hillside community was getting

very worried about a prolonged drought during what should have been the June growing season. Finally even a stream called Old Duncan, that usually sent its spray high as it went its sparkling way over the transparency of rocks, for the first time in known history lay dried out. Then, with the smell of the parched earth reaching for rain in a need past pride, on their own initiative the neighborhood farmers held a prayer meeting. And they laid it on the line.

"Lord," said a burly man, coming to his feet and gazing upward in direct appeal, "we're bad off for rain. Now, don't send us a drivin' storm that'll wash all the crops into Old Duncan. Just send a gentle three-day zizzle-zozzel." And the rains came.

Even the old mountain hymns have a personal poignancy, such as "The Ninety and Nine." It's a wonderful song, the way a country congregation swings into it low and swings into it high, and wails its pity.

> "There were ninety and nine, that safely lay,
> In the shelter o-of the shepherd's fold.
> But one was *out* in the hills away,
> *Away*, away, far *out* in the hills so cold."

Then there are those highlanders like the woman who felt she had a few more knotty problems of every day than she could well handle, without worrying about the hills beyond. "Hit gives me the headache to think." It apparently seemed simpler to inscribe optimistically on a hilltop slab marker: "Gone to Heaven to be an angel."

We know a crossroads storekeeper who takes a view detached, but not indifferent, as he expounded one afternoon when we stopped in after a walk for a Coke.

"With all the churches there are, nobody yet has figured out the proper way to get baptized. The Baptists think that immersion's the thing to clean you up. A little sprinklin' don't count. The Presbyterians believe in baptism or be damned, even babies. Why, if there's one pure thing in God's green world, it's an innocent newborn babe. If there aren't enough Methodists around to run the place, they'll take a few sinners to help chip in. For that matter, if you chip in right good to any denomination, you'll ascend straight through to glory with a crown big as a bucket."

His knowledge of Catholicism was limited to noting that the priest drank all the wine himself, and stood with his back to you. "Now, that's against my early training. When a man talks to me, I want him to look me in the eye."

Best of all he liked the Quaker service. "One time a Friend—he looked like a clever man—stopped in at the store and bought some things; nothin' fancy—a hoe, harness straps, a bolt of black linsey-woolsey, that sort of stuff and makin' sure the quality was good. I cottoned to the fellow, and one thing leadin' to another as it does, while I was helpin' him load up his buggy, I asked him what the Quaker church was like. He kindly twinkled and said why didn't I come out next Sunday and see.

"Well, it was just a little wood church way out in the country and when I finally got it located, there was my customer in his broad-brimmed black hat waitin' for me. He invited me in and I sat with him on the men's side. Right away I could see that the Quakers hold a service peculiar to themselves. The men—they keep their hats on—sit on one side, and the women in their black bonnets sit together on the other side. Nothin' happened for five or ten minutes and I was gettin' figgity, wonderin' why they didn't get started."

Yet he'd never forget how impressed he was by the way the quiet of that service soaked into him like rain into dry ground. Directly he wasn't in a hurry, about anything. It was nice there while he waited.

"Then an elder stood up and spoke. And what he said made damned good common sense. Another five minutes went by before the spirit moved a woman to rise and say a few words. I don't recall quite how she said it, but the idea was that just because trouble knocked at the door you didn't have to ask it in and set it in a chair. By and by a few others would stand and talk a while, then they'd all sit quiet a while. They just had themselves a time! There's a lot of mankind built into the Quakers."

Sincerely though he respected the peace-loving Friends, he did not join their faith or any other. "Fact is," he said comfortably, "I'm not much for prayin' in damp churches."

Formalized good is not always good, as I well knew. "That's right," he agreed earnestly. His eyes and the fleshly quality of his face suggested that his had not been a small life. It had included tolerance and good humor, and a dexterity for avoiding anything that might interfere with them. Just the same, as highlanders in earnest conversation are apt to do, not letting either the best or the worst of themselves settle to the bottom, to become stagnant, eventually to dam the flow, he went on.

"I got to studyin' about somethin' just the other day, though. Maybe it was because I read it when I was just a green country boy and at that religious age. Anyway, it hit me about as hard as anything ever has. One time a Hebrew Prophet—Micah, his name was—said somethin' I remember to this day. Likely you know it too." We didn't, not the whole of it; not the mountain beginning.

" 'Arise, contend thou before the mountains, and let the hills hear thy voice. . . . And what doth the Lord require of thee, but to deal justly, and to love mercy, and to walk humbly with thy God?' It's a wonder, when all the churches preach the selfsame thing, they can't get together on that one point at least and just have a joyful time. Oh well"—the crossroads storekeeper rested an elbow on the cash register, the fingers of his practical hand falling with the grace of acceptance—"it takes a long time to learn."

In a high valley in the North Carolina Blue Ridge, where the mountains, changing with every season, every shift of sun and shadow, are so greatly beautiful your soul widens to take them in, there is a little chapel. Its architecture is symbolic of something unfinished but of incalculable possibilites.

Its side windows are plain, so that the blackberry bushes and laurel outside are a part of its feeling of being at one with all things. The single art-glass window is at the front, behind the pulpit: a young Christ and a child in royal colors.

Chestnut bark covers the inside walls, and the ceiling is so simple an arch as the stable of Bethlehem might have had. Whole young trunks of sapling chestnut trees, crossed like the swords of many truths, emphasize the arch, an intricate lacery of natural materials. The hardness of each kneeling bench is a reminder of its being an object of search that leads in devious ways. The odor of an answer seems in the church's smell, sweet and old—from the wood; from the aging of worshiping minds of those who have partaken and given there.

It is a good place to go alone. You feel a reluctance to leave. You want to linger, as you want to linger in the touch of peace. But coming out onto the little stone porch, the air changes. It quickens and sharpens—still sweet, but with the wild sweetness of earth and rain.

Jollification

Mary Burleson age 72 Feb 3 did 1907
she ware a lady good Criston she lik
everibodi

EVEN though you are a mountaineer only by adop-
tion, if ever you have once loved the ugliness of a small mountain
village knocked up carelessly around a broad place in a bad road,
you go back and back to it. And if ever you've gone on an over-
night camping party in weather that would give you pneumonia
if you had to be out in it in the city, you literally almost break
your neck to go do the same fool thing again.

Weather somehow never seems to be a matter of slightest consideration in these camping parties. Somebody gets the idea for
one, and the affair goes off with all the good and bad points of
lack of planning. Everybody collects whatever blankets they
think they can get away with without too much argument. Somebody brings a skillet and somebody else an ax. The mood stays
spontaneously high but the food is apt to be uncertain. Larders
are raided for whatever cakes and bread happen to be on hand,
and chickens are sacrificed. If it's that time of year, there are
roasting ears and tomatoes. If it's later, there are peaches and
apples.

The crowd collects at the store and a harum-scarum check-up
is made of whatever else might be needed. Then the party is
off—in vehicles as haphazardly assembled as the other necessi-
ties. Mountain drivers seem naturally possessed with a reckless
skill that swings you out to the edges and squeals you around

curves, all on the bland theory that there is no other car in the country. Any tired idea you may have had that about as much life was left in you as in a woody turnip and that nothing exciting would ever happen to you again departs speedily with the first half mile.

You drive as far up the chosen mountain as you can, and farther than any outsider from the world of wide highways thinks possible. Finally, even the driver agrees that he's gone as far as his springs will take him and he parks the car among oaks and boulders. Everybody piles out. Before you quite leave civilization altogether, some stalwart picks up a rail from the last outpost of farm fence to start the fire. He shoulders the fence rail and leads the way up.

Wind and mist and darkness, and mountains of white rock rising up out of the darkness. You go on climbing; clambering over an unannounced boulder in the path; by some miracle not slipping on pine needles off the narrow path down into a few thousand feet of fog before you'd hit the first treetop; coming finally to solid footing—a great rock not quite to the top. A stocky balsam, a wind-runted laurel, some huckleberries stand their ground in a crevice on the rock making their single, lonely sound. But below, millions of trees are making the soft rainy noises of wind blowing the fog off leaves.

The mountain fog is not a dank fog that hangs heavy. It is swiftly moving, constantly changing—now revealing enough strange light to promise everything, the next instant wiping it out.

The fog in your face, not too cold. The smoke from the fire built in the shelter of rock sweet in your nostrils. The night sky is stormy—but not so black, not so everlasting, not so almighty as the black peak.

Everything familiar and trite and tired is rolled up behind you someplace. The world is new and raw and beautiful and there isn't a mistake in it. You have come eagerly, needing this.

As for a part in every-day community life, there is the choir practice. The volunteer village choir is apt to be the kind that by a slip of punctuation was announced in a Sunday bulletin as "Lord have mercy The Choir!" But somehow noise you make yourself always sounds all right.

The last practice I went to started off horribly. Everybody was feeling his way along, and the soprano section was trying notes too high for it. The pianist, a local woman who lived in a slab house set close to the road in front so it wouldn't miss anything and held up in back by stilts, turned on the piano stool and peered at us over her pinch-nose glasses.

"It don't seem to gee right," she criticized.

So we went over the first part again. It still was not all it should be.

"There's something the matter with my ears, our singing, or the man who made this thing up," decided the minister's wife, a young woman with merry eyes and healthy cheeks.

"Let's try just that one line, 'Let His mercies extend,' " suggested a teacher who sang alto, "and see what makes that funny gap that always comes in there."

"That's middle G," explained the pianist. "It don't work. Now, go through the whole thing and see if you can't stop churnin' on that 'Sabbath day ne'er spent in vain.' "

We went through the whole thing again, and toward the end began to nudge each other in triumph, and everybody gave all they had to the last three notes.

"Well," the pianist was pleased. "Our end is one thing they won't be able to criticize."

"For once," said the doctor, a quiet tower of a man who sang bass and kept the choir going, "I believe we almost got together."

Everybody was proud, everybody wanted to do the ending again. There was a strange satisfaction in the mild humor and wholesome effort of that midweek choir practice for the Sunday services in a little country church.

And you have not laughed for a long time, really, until you have gotten red in the face from the effort of trying the light-toed, loose-kneed shuffling grace of the "play-party" dances to the sawing of a fiddle—too busy to notice that you've lost your dignity and too exhausted afterward from breathlessness and laughing to care.

Many a solid male has suffered in dancing class—hauled there, needless to say, by his wife, who for the past few years has found him not so light on her feet. Sometimes the solid citizen can stand just so much of it.

That solid citizen, however, finds nothing of the piffling or effete to irk him as the caller of the mountain square dance bawls out, "Big Ring!" Awkward bodies grown stiff with the slow labor of highland farms slip into easy repose. Limbs bend freely, and presently, as the fiddler, who has been staring off into space with absolutely no expression whatsoever on his face, gets down to the serious business of whanging the life out of his instrument, the solid citizen finds himself light-footing it with the other gents "to the center and right straight back." He finds he is a good dancer —there is force to his short, swift steps, a nonchalance to his light smooth spring from step to step. Or so he imagines. At any rate, he swings his lady home like hell a-hootin' for sideways, and whistles the tune all the way back to the inn.

The folk songs and dances of our frontier people who carved an empire out of the vastness of trackless wilderness are enjoying a rapid renascence. They are springing to life with virgin force in the hundreds of regional Appalachian annual festivals. The Old Time Fiddlers World Championship is an Easter specialty of Union Grove, North Carolina.

A real old-time fiddler, could he have returned, likely would have breathed an astounded, "Thunderin' 'ell!" at all the cars with 1968 license plates from far states; at some of the outfits worn by contestants tuning up—plastic motorcycle helmets, beads and beards, flower-children costumes. Yet, on looking them over, he might have felt right at home, the frontier fiddler with red stripes on his high boots, his blue homespun jeans matching his ham-smacker coat, a red and white spotted calfskin vest tanned with the hairs left on, a straw hat, and his instrument tied up in a big flowered handkerchief. His composure regained,

9   Green hills on either side of a winding
road mark off far distances.

10   A gate, a bridge . . . the time and loneliness to link the present with the past.

11

Lookout Mountain, Tennessee, a battlesite of the Civil War, when the
mountain people bespoke a nation ripped asunder.

12   *"Joy be with you while you stay*
And peace go with you on your way."

he would likely have said laconically of the fourteen thousand furriners spilling over into the fields and woods around the tiny town, "Right smart crowd."

In several of the mountain festivals the age of chivalry is coming alive in the form of jousting, straight out of King Arthur's Knights of the Round Table—or almost straight, having undergone certain revisions since it was brought into the American Colonies.

Jousting is becoming increasingly popular in Virginia and South Carolina. Maryland has lately claimed it has been popular there since 1634, and in 1962 made it the state's official sport. Evidently West Virginia has always taken jousting for granted. Only comparatively recently has it become an annual event. In the old days it was just a commonplace sport. A tourney was held in anybody's pasture on any Saturday afternoon that neighborhood men were in the mood to match skills. And, of course, every rider had his own custom-made lance.

They still do, as my husband and I learned when we went to see the Moorefield Tournament in the South Branch country.

The owner of our motel, whose office walls were lined with a family collection of antique firearms, was more a man of quiet action than talk. But on hearing why we were there, to see the Moorefield Tournament, he courteously showed us the lance he had used in his tournament-riding youth. He took it down off a storeroom shelf that we might get the feel of it in our hands. Its surprising lightness, he explained, was because it had been carved out of pine. An uncle, who was a good carpenter, had made it for him. Fully eight feet in length and perfectly balanced, its metal tip had been fined to a wicked-looking point— for a very practical purpose, as we were to see.

The Moorefield Tournament, scheduled to start at six o'clock on Saturday evening, was the entertaining wind-up of the town's annual Poultry Festival. It was held at the open-field end of a short side street. The arena was a roped-off grassy space beside the carnival set up for the festival. We arrived early enough to watch the gathering crowd of town and countryside people—and we had grandstand seats! Our motel host thoughtfully had backed his truck up to a center place along the rope, and there we sat with other new-found friends.

And if you had to imagine the waving of colorful banners, the blare of trumpets, the tumultuous shouts as plumed knights in shining armor galloped down the lists in clattering collision, jousting Mountain State style certainly was not wanting in excitement, or tradition either.

The Marshal, as the master of ceremonies is entitled, took his stand on the tail gate of a red truck next to us and started the tourney off with fanfare. He impressively unrolled a long scroll and, in stentorian tones, read the tournament instructions to each mounted knight who presented himself as an entry to the lists.

The instructions were noble stuff. "Sir Knight of Spruce Knob, I charge you, as in the days of Sir Lancelot when gallant knights rode down into the green valley, abide by the code of chivalry. Remember that the blood of the fearless English, Scots, Normans, and French flows through your veins. Hold fast to your integrity that you may bring to your maiden fair the laurels of a true hero, the love of a pure heart. Be ever courageous, loyal, and polite. Conduct yourself with honor in victory or defeat . . . Sir Knight of Charles Town, I charge you . . . Sir Knight of Whiskey Creek . . ." Thus each young knight in shining white shirt was appraised of his moral responsibility.

Then, the tempo built up, the Marshal raised the capable flat of a hand for the starting signal, his voice thunderous. "Little John, Sir Knight of Clay Hill, charge!"

From that instant on, no fourteen jousters (counting a straw-hatted youngster on a pony) were ever more thrillingly watched. On the track, placed an exact seventy-five feet apart, were three wooden arches. From the center cross pole of each arch a wire dangled. As the tournament progressed, there were triggered, in succession, from each wire black and white rings of diminishing sizes, ranging from one and a half inches in diameter to half an inch.

Each knight's objective was to charge these rings and impale them at full gallop. After three tries the triumphant knight who rode up to the judges' bench with the most rings threaded onto the metal tip of his lance would be privileged crowner of his chosen queen. The three runners-up would crown the queen's court. Also, it was very important that the knights keep their lances balanced at all times during the tourney, whether riding or holding their prancing horses in check waiting their next turn —otherwise, the rings already gained would slip off.

It was a display of superb horsemanship, made all the more extraordinary by the course being somewhat shorter than a football field and slightly wider than a bowling alley. The contestants rode at breakneck speed, reins in their left hand, lance poised in the right, at eye level, as though sighting a rifle on the briefly spaced dangling rings. The crowd cheered and sighed, and caught its breath, and laughed.

And then the tournament was over, save for the grand finale. On a platform behind the Ferris wheel, each of the four victorious young knights in gallant turn placed a flowered crown on the head of his fair lady, took a formal step backward, and bowed from lean waist to the queen and her court, all four of whom wore shorts. But then, probably Maid Marian too wore the country dress of her day.

The Marshal, his duty done, hustled past us saying something about having to catch a derned colt that had slipped its halter. The most spontaneously cheered-for-effort hero of the event, the youngster who missed every single ring and on his last try dropped his lance, rode past consolingly patting his pony. Our host, ruddy face aglow, voiced pretty sure hope that his own freckled-faced little grandson would soon be trying a hand at the lance he was keeping for that very purpose.

Homeward bound, we carried away with us the enlivening feeling that even a short time in the mountains can lend.

A Mighty Pretty Story

popelers is springing green apri 1 1901

LETHA came from back-country Fish Creek. Her world there wasn't very big. The sun came up over a clean hill line back of the barn and went down behind the wooded roughs that rose up out of a winding valley. But it was wide, wide in living lore.

Since she became, briefly, a part of our West Virginia household in answer to a Help Wanted ad in the local paper after our own young housekeeper left to be married, we assumed she would act as maid. A mistaken asumption, as Letha made immediately clear. She was merely obligingly "helping out." Not that she said so, it was just there, that sense of equality so typical of her mountain kind. On her first evening in the house she sat with the family in the living room until, politely stifling a yawn with her fingertips, she said, "Well, if you folks will excuse me, I think I'll go to bed."

Also, it was soon evident that Letha was a twentieth-century product of what has long been known as "the land of do without." Indeed, one of the few times she ever had ridden in an automobile was with her more affluent cousin Elmer over a road more familiarly traveled by wagon. It was a memorable experience in several ways. "Over all them rocks up that little old run, I'll tell you I was scared afore I started almost. But Elmer just had a picnic." That is, until Elmer ran afoul of a tree, bringing an abrupt end to the joy-ride and landing Letha into the novelty of the so-called office of a neighborhood doctor. The ingenious medic patched up a scalp gash by implanting a metal plate.

Otherwise, she was as hale and hearty a young woman as I've ever known; a ruddy face with all the life of earth and animal in it—in no way a dainty woman or at all unbeautiful, as health and pleasant laughter create a beauty that draws even the unwary to it. At the outset, when something "tickled her so good," her outright merriment, accompanied by lifting one leg and giving a resounding slap to her knee, tended to bring my dignified husband straight up out of his quiet evening chair three startled rooms away. But then, as Letha explained, she didn't look right when she wasn't a-laughin'; she looked "sanctified."

And once she very nearly did. The transfiguration occurred one summer morning apropos of her mentioning that "castor oil just winds me up." Nevertheless, apparently it was used as a cure-all in her house, where her three children had arrived safe and sound sans benefit of medical science. Ample arms crossed, she leaned comfortably back against the kitchen sink and told about the day her first one, Richard, came.

"I was up afore light, to get my man off to help a neighbor with the hayin'. It looked to be a pretty day, so I made up a big batch of lye soap and washed every rag rug in the place. The sun was high by then, and la, them rugs were a sight to see, a-flappin' in the wind where I'd hung them out on the fence to dry. Then I mixed up a crock of sausage and was fixin' to bake a light cake when I commenced to feel kinda funny. My sister Ruth's little girl was visitin' me that day and I said, 'Lula Bell, if you ain't scared (it was comin' on toward dusk), I wish you'd go tell Mom I'd like to see her.'

"Lula Bell said she wasn't scared, and directly Mom and my sister Ruth both come down. We set around on the porch and talked and laughed like common for a spell, then I said, 'Mom, I wish you'd put some water on to heat.' Mom give me a look. 'Now what's the matter with you?' 'Nothin',' I said. 'I just want to wash my dirty feet a little.' Mom said, 'I knowed there was somethin' the matter with you.' But my man never knowed a thing about it till he come in home that night and heard the baby holler!"

A kitchen window beside Letha was letting in the freshness of this summer's morning on a shaft of windy sun that fell across the hearty mountain face. And in that moment she was lovely.

"Mis' Hannum, I'll never forget it, the way he picked that youngun up in his arms, then smiled down proud and said, 'Well, you don't take yore looks from no stranger.' "

Letha spoke often, with earnest awe, of her first-born, then thirteen. "I tell you, that boy's a man. He's just an all-around man, that boy is."

All in all, the Richard saga seemed fairly well summed up in her grandfather's words of natural wisdom, respectfully quoted. "Like begets like in spite of the Devil."

Thereafter her first-born's sire was dropped from mention, either directly or indirectly. But the grandfather was frequently with us, striding through the ballads his forebears had brought from far lands across, and that Letha sang to our children at bedtime. They weren't exactly what little girls were hearing at the beginning of the Second World War. Nevertheless, the storied songs of long-ago people seemed justified by the unlikelihood of the children ever again hearing them so kindly rendered with such nasal authenticity. And they listened in fascination, as did I, for Letha certainly could "flirt a tune" with gusto, as befitted her zestful choices.

No melancholy accounts of plaintive sweetness for her. Rather, she leaned toward those of unvarnished moralistic value. One of her favorites was about an indiscreet lady who might have been lost forever in commonality had it not been for the uncommon fate of her lover. And it had a lively air.

There was a lovely lady, in London she did dwell.
She was the Captain's wife, and the tailor loved her well.
The Captain had not been three hours, I'm shore it was not four,
Till there come a knocking, knocking at the door.

Alas, the cowardly tailor made his hasty hiding hole the Captain's cannily forgotten sea chest. The mighty Captain, no fool, heaved the chest overboard into the deep dark sea where, he declared, "You'll raise no little tailor boys for me."

On her weekend off, Letha was called for by her current "friend," a mortician who announced his presence by honking his horn from the driveway. Evidently he was a more responsible sort than her joy-riding cousin Elmer, judging by her commendation overheard during a lengthy phone conversation: "Homer, I always know where you're at, Homer." The compliment so sufficiently covered the whole field of dependability, it became a household saying.

And Letha continued her evensongs for our children, the ballads she'd tapped her feet to many a night as a child when her grandfather had sung them. Whatever the cultural force of these country songs on Merrie Olde England, as they came to us via Fish Creek they carried the impact of energy directed and released. One piece of Fish Creek folk was particularly intriguing, both for its verve and content. Though basically it expressed youth's timeless threat to dogmatic repression, combined with a very modern feeling of freedom to its rhythm, it had a form rare in balladry. At least I'd never heard it before, nor have I since. Pleased by my interest, Letha offered to "word it" for me. And she generously did, writing it down painstakingly on school tablet paper, adding a penciled note hoping that I'd "get a good laugh out of it."

It gets off to an attention-jolting start—a line of archaic jargon with a hard, thrusting beat. For repetitive dramatic build-up, the singer may emphasize the beat by interjecting the jargon whenever the varying mood strikes. And so it starts, the ancient song of love and war:

Lo lee lo-ah, lo lee lo!

They were riding from the church, returning home again,
When they met her dear old father, and seven armored men.

"Ho," said the father, "you are a soldier's wife.
Well, for that misbehavior I'll shorely have yore life."

Lo lee lo-ah, lo lee lo!

"Ho," said the soldier, "I don't like no such prattle,
Even though I am the bridegroom, and not prepared for battle."

He drew his sword and pistol, and this was caused to rattle.
The lady held the horses, while her husband went to battle.

The first man he come to, he struck him through the main,
The second man he come to, he had him strictly slain.

Lo lee lo-ah, lo lee lo!

"Hold," said the old man, "and do not be so bold.
You may have my daughter—and ten thousand pounds of gold."

"Fight on," said the lady. "The portion is too small.
You kill the old man, and then we'll have it all."

Lo lee lo-ah, lo lee lo!

"Hold," said the old man, "pray do not be so bold!
You may have my daughter—and all of my gold."

Then up to their horses, and homeward they did ride.
And oh, what a wedding feast that old man did provide.

He called him his son, and he called him his heir.
He didn't do it 'cause he loved him, he done it in mortal f-are!

Lo lee lo-ah, lo lee lo!

So hark, ye fair damsels of riches and great store.
Never slight a soldier boy although he may be pore.

For by this tale, it's shorely plain to see
That he'll fight for his sweetheart, as quick as liberty.

Lo lee lo-ah, lo lee lo!

Soon the red hollyhocks were almost as high as the children's
little white playhouse in the back yard and, praise be, our good
friend and housekeeper Mary unexpectedly came back, with her
dashing Polish husband. Yet in her quite different way Letha too
has a lasting place in our lives. Periodically she still calls us from
her own chatty phone to ask fondly about the girls and to say
that all her folks "are doing gaily." And just before she departed,

she made a return gesture of the hospitality that she warmly maintains she enjoyed with us. She relayed my pleasure in his songs to Grandpa, who sent an invitation in reply. He'd be God proud to have us take supper with him.

Inadvertently, Letha had given us an inkling of what to expect. She'd been so delighted to discover on a basement shelf a coal-oil lamp, kept there for emergency use on windy nights when the electricity was inclined to go off on our country hill, that I had given it to her. The very next weekend she took the lamp home with her and gave it to Grandpa. The present was a brilliant success. On her Monday-morning return she reported cheerfully, "He's got the house all lit up like a saloon."

As the crow flies, it was only a few ridges away. As the winding road went, the stars were out before we made our final approach, up a steep slope that was scarcely more than a footpath. But the children loved it—they leaned far out of the car windows to feel how wide and quiet the night was.

The lamp was in tactful prominence on the supper table. If the meal itself was unremarkable, not so the host as the evening went on—a spare old man sitting erect on a hickory chair at one side of the soapstone fireplace and throwing a long shadow on the log wall. A soft-spoken man with an alerting face. By the flickering light of fire flame, his long white beard and craggy brows, shielding thin-lidded eyes the blue of misty mountains with the sun behind them, gave him striking resemblance to a mild Moses. Actually, his name was John Wesley.

Aside from being venerable of mien and name, he had the distinction of being one of the very few Civil War veterans left alive to tell the tale. But Grandpa was a disappointment on the score of giving forth with firsthand accounts of heroic deeds and stirring action. He did obligingly take down from a wall peg a battered Rebel cap, and with a gnarled forefinger point out where a bullet had gone in one side and out the other. "Then," he said, laconically replacing the relic, "I picked up a murderous weapon." And that seemed about all there was to tell of the incident.

Besides, he was just a shirt-tail boy when he joined up, lied about his age to get in, and by then the trouble was almost over. But he was in it long enough to be impressed by a sad thing. A lot of the men who'd come down off the ridges couldn't read or write. And if there was one thing that meant more than anything in the world to a lonesome soldier, it was a letter from home. So if anybody at home could write, a soldier would get somebody else to read his letter to him.

"We were mean, ornery heathen," he said of himself and his comrades. But they did one good thing in that fray, leastwise all and every man did who had his head set on square. They swore that when they climbed back home to the hills—if they weren't called to the City of their Fathers before they got there—they'd build log schoolhouses and skin their youngins alive if they didn't go and get themselves educated. And the men planned how they'd get primpted up and take their womenfolks to the spelling bees and entertainments held nights in the schoolhouses.

But in aftermath drudgery, any such upward yearning was only a pointless, smashing inward violence. In the dulling course of time, when there was no longer height or depth to the spirit, the yearning was leveled too.

For Letha's children, however, a sky-high world of limitless possibilities was in the making. The following week they were entering a spelling contest at their red-brick country schoolhouse, and afterward there would be a pie social. Letha was excitedly ready for the event. She'd bought a white taffeta gown to wear. And she'd decorated her pie box with purple crepe paper.

Her grandfather listened with interest, although he didn't figure on going. He reckoned he'd got all the learning he'd ever have, in the war. One fellow in his mess—he had the kindest eyes and they didn't deceive him none—for a while there held a sort of school. He could read Latin, and once he read them a mighty pretty story about a man named Caesar. He wrote some of it down for John Wesley.

The old John Wesley got up slowly from his chair. Slowly he picked up the lamp from the table and carried it into the adjoining dark of another room. When he reappeared, he had a scrap of folded paper in his hand, which he took to the fireplace where he placed the lamp on the stone mantelpiece.

He spoke no word for several moments, but something about him commanded attention; something remindful of balsam that spears straight and starkly thrives above the ordinary timber line. He unfolded the paper with care, for the flyleaf torn from a small book had grown brittle with the years. Then he bent slightly down, holding his keepsake close to the smoking light of lamp and fire, the better to see its fading writing, although he had never learned to read what the writing said. But in the room's shadowy stillness he seemed to be hearing again the thin scratch of a fine pen.

When he straightened, his face was alive with the pretty story on the torn page that still lay open in his work-worn hand.

"Caesar got into the flatlands of England," he said thoughtfully, "but he never conquered the hills."

The World Is New

Jacob Carpenter start colrado Jul 3 1888
com home Jan 1889

YOU thought you had remembered. But you find you had forgotten. You had forgotten the power, the power and the peace; the uselessness of petty things. The freedom!

Perhaps it is a yearning of the mind and body for a temporary suspension of all thought and feeling that takes you back to the mountains. Over after-dinner coffee recently a man much involved and harassed with international affairs said that there was just one thing he wanted to do. He wanted time to sit and just spit. Everyone in the room laughed, with a mixture of understanding and wistfulness.

Mountains are one of the better places to sit—and spit, if you wish. Either way, you can sit in a sunny place above the cascade of green falling to a ribbon of road in the valley, not thinking of anything much, and have a very good time at it.

And once on a moonlit night we were sitting on the cliff edge of Wiseman's View with two of our North Carolina friends who had been away for a while, one to France and the other to China, and were now home to stay. Across the soft dark of the gorge, the mountains in moonlight were only a suggestion of greatness. The Linville River crashing against rocks was too far below to hear on its inevitable way to the sea. There was no wind that night, only a gentle sharpness to the air, like the feeling of being rightly alive without stress.

In a clear quiet came a drift of singing. A group of picnickers

around a campfire on a wide flat rock a ways behind us were
singing the ballads their people had sung for generations of evenings. It was the sort of thing that makes you smile quickly in
wonder, for here they were again, the old songs that should have
gone long ago. A teasing song, one of them was, with the light of
young insolence taking the sting out:

> It's a beautiful life on the ocean,
> It's a beautiful life on the sea.
> It's a beautiful life on the ocean,
> And my love, I waited for thee.
>
> Seven long years I've been married,
> And I wish I'd lived an old maid.
> My husband goes down to the barroom,
> And now he won't work at his trade.
>
> I've a little ship on the ocean,
> All mounted in silver and gold.
> But before I'd marry again,
> That ship would be anchored and sold.

And the picnickers laughed delightedly at their own impu-
dence, their own delight in the high wide ease of the moonlight
that brought them very close. Without stress, that was the new-
ness in a night of time-old things, even as the tempo of their cliff
singing changed to provocative tenderness of question and answer:

> I gave my love a cherry without a stone
> I gave my love a chicken without a bone
> I gave my love a ring without an end
> I gave my love a baby with no cryin'.
>
> How can there be a cherry without a stone?
> How can there be a chicken without a bone?
> How can there be a ring without an end?
> How can there be a baby with no cryin' ?
>
> A cherry when it's bloomin', it has no stone.
> A chicken when it's pippin', it has no bone.

A ring when it's rollin', it has no end,
A baby when it's sleepin', has no cryin'.

Nor do you have to climb to great heights. You can ascend the
mildest hill in sight, maybe the rise back of the village school or
by your lodge. But, as the mountain woman said when she had
occasion to try to figure out the sorry sense of the world, "A little
height makes a sight of difference in the way a body sees things."
When you can get above confusion and look to the quiet strength
and beauty of the hills, with each going on into the next and the
next till they take on sureness and sweep, you grow somehow not
afraid. It is as though you have ascended to some altitude of
yourself, to some inner reserve of endurance you had forgotten
about, or perhaps never knew was there.

And you can walk down a mountain road when the sky is a
glittering blue and the air is fresh, or you can take a side road
that leads by a creek with forget-me-nots along its banks and you
need not climb at all.

Of color, there is a squander of it from blooming April to
golden October. The winter snows offer rose and purple peaks.
And in the bewilderment of man-made destruction, it is good to
look at so sure a thing as greening rhododendron shoots and say
in simple wonder, "Look!"

For smell, if you've ever known the aromatic spice of cool
mountain woods, laurel and teaberry and pine, and old logs with
their sweetness still in them, then you can understand the heart-
felt utterance of a returned mountain man who fervently declared,
"I'd ruther be a knot on a log up hyur than the mayor of the city
down yonder."

Mountain people leave, but some come back. They come back,
those with their roots deep in these changing mountains that go
further than the eye can reach, further than the accounting of
time. And others come back who chanced upon the mountains at
some magic time or place that took hold on their thoughts and on
their lives.

And in each new generation there will be an adventuring few

who feel the same primal draw that the first seekers knew to mountains rising like a misty dream of greatness; a greatness of being, beyond selfless self. Even though that yearning be found only in the spirit's pulling upward, it brings wondrous things to mind of circles completed but not ended.